True Tales of WENTZVILLE

The Early Years

Gerry Matlock, Lois Kessler
and Kathy Weindel

The History Press

Published by The History Press
An imprint of Arcadia Publishing
Charleston, SC
www.historypress.com

Front cover, top: People waiting at the Wentzville Railroad Station for its passenger train. As you can see from the number of people, the passenger service was widely used. *Wentzville Community Historic Society (WCHS) Collection. Bottom*: An 1870s locomotive, no. 218, with a caboose and several passenger cars. *WCHS Collection. Back cover*: The Wentzville train tracks north of the depot (*left*), showing what is now East Allen Street and several of the businesses and stores from the past. This street was also called Railroad Street, Allen and North Main in the past. Across from the depot and two sets of tracks is a round building (*center left*) that stored chemicals to help fight fires. The top of the round building also served as a bandstand. *WCHS Collection.*

First published 2025

Manufactured in the United States

ISBN 9781467159234

Library of Congress Control Number: 2025935720

Notice: The information in this book is true and complete to the best of our knowledge. It is offered without guarantee on the part of the authors or The History Press. The authors and The History Press disclaim all liability in connection with the use of this book.

Contents

Acknowledgements

Writing and researching a book is a team effort. The time involved affects family and friends, and if you are lucky, they understand your commitment.

The Wentzville Community Historical Society (WCHS) would like to thank Gerry Matlock for graciously giving us permission to use the Wentzville articles and research he did in the 1970s. Thank you to volunteers Kathy Weindel and Lois Kessler for their research and for writing various articles and updating some of Gerry's articles. And thank you to our mapmaker, Allyn Benkowich.

Thank you to the archivist and researchers at the Missouri Historical Society, the Missouri History Museum, the State Historical Society of Missouri at Columbia and at St. Louis, the Missouri Library and Research Center, National Park Services at the Gateway Arch, Duke University, the Montgomery County Historical Society, the Rubenstein Library at Duke University, the Missouri State Archives and the St. Charles County Historical Society.

Thanks also go to Ben Gibson and Joe Gartrell, commissioning editors at The History Press, for their advice and encouragement as we worked on the book.

But most importantly, we need to thank and say how grateful we are for our volunteer Kathy Beckmann, who has worked tirelessly on this project for over a year, keeping us on track and helping with research. All the things she has done for this project are too numerous to list. This book would still be a dream without her work and dedication.

The Wentzville Community Historical Society is a nonprofit 501(c)(3). All royalties from the sale of this book will go to WCHS to help further our mission, "To preserve and share our history with the public," and our vision, "Our history available to everyone."

Introduction

On the day man told the story of his life to man, history was born.
—Alfred de Vigny

In 1975, Wentzville Mayor Don Sheets appointed a committee to plan activities to celebrate the bicentennial of the United States of America in 1976. The committee got busy. They planned parades and other events, they buried a time capsule and, as a committee, they learned the importance of knowing our history. An outgrowth of that committee was the formation of the Wentzville Community Historical Society (WCHS). As a society, we represent the western half of St. Charles County, and we have been collecting memories and materials about this area for almost fifty years.

For some of our members, the history of this area has become a passion, and they have devoted hours to the pursuit of learning about the past. One such person was WCHS founding member Gerry Matlock. He interviewed older citizens; he tracked down people who had lived here but moved away; he found and gathered photos; and, most importantly, he wrote about what he found and published his findings in articles for the *Wentzville Union*, the *Messenger-Tribune* and the *St. Charles County Record*.

It has long been the dream of WCHS to publish the stories that Gerry wrote in a book. When approached, Gerry graciously gave us permission. However, as we worked on the book, we realized that there were so many stories to tell. This area has had a wealth of interesting happenings and people. We started to dig deeper. The book as presented contains some of Gerry's articles, of which some have been updated to include research the society has done. We soon realized that we had more stories than our book could hold, so the decision was made to talk about the early years, the founding years.

For various reasons, Wentzville is one of the fastest-growing cities in the United States. Our hope is that new residents will enjoy the stories and become involved in preserving the history of their new city and that citizens who have been here for a long time will appreciate what has come before and lend their memories of growing up in the area.

Author Hilary Mantel said, "The past changes a little every time we retell it." We have done our best to capture the good, the bad and the ugly; we believe it is all important. Oscar Wilde said that "history is merely gossip," and businessman Eckhard Pfeiffer said, "Today we are making history." Pfeiffer's words remind us that our today will, in the future, be someone else's history.

The newspapers in the past were like Facebook today. They told us who came to town, who left, who visited who, who was related to who. They told us about parties and who attended, what the bride wore, who moved, who bought a new stove—they told us everything. They were invaluable in our research. We could go back 50, 100, 150 years. We worry about researchers in the future. Today, almost everyone's life is on Facebook, but we worry that in the future, it won't be available to researchers. For that reason, we encourage everyone to document their family history, write their stories down, join our Write Your Story class, document those pictures so at some point they aren't just thrown in the trash because no one knows who they're of.

We hope you enjoy the stories we have shared, and we hope you will feel free to share with us your family tree and photos, so we can add them to our archives. Meanwhile, we are back to researching about more people in our area.

Chapter 1

History and Growth of Western St. Charles County

History and Growth of Western St. Charles County

By Gerry Matlock
Originally published in the Wentzville Union, *April 23, 1975*
Edited by Lois Kessler, August 2024

A substantial amount of chapter 1 was obtained from the 1885 book *History of St. Charles, Montgomery and Warren Counties, Missouri*, which is now in the public domain.* This book, published by the St. Louis National Historical Company, contains important information about the early settlers of St. Charles County along with the counties of Montgomery and Warren in the state of Missouri.

> The first settlements by white men in the State of Missouri were made at St. Genevieve and New Bourbon about 1735. St. Louis was founded by Pierre Laclede Liguest in 1764. The next settlement was made at Potosi in 1765 where a lead mine was discovered. The first settlement in Northern Missouri was at St. Charles in 1769. The settlement was named Les Petites Cotes meaning Little Hills, which it retained until 1784. The town was founded by a Frenchman called

* Available at Missouri Digital Heritage, https://mdh.contentdm.oclc.org/digital/collection/mocohist/id/26291.

Louis Blanchette surnamed "The Hunter," who built the first fort and established a military post. He located on the present town site of the city of St. Charles on the Missouri River and died about the year 1793. He was commissioned by the Governor of Upper Louisiana to establish a post here under the Spanish government, and was, until the date of his death, its first civil and military governor.

The country, at the time of Blanchette's arrival, was an unbroken wilderness, inhabited by animals and Native Americans, who roamed at will through forest and prairie in this region, except in the immediate vicinity of the military post at St. Charles, until 1795. A few houses had, in the meantime, been built at St. Charles, numbering about a dozen, between the years 1769 and 1791, but these were the inferior, temporary huts of the commandant, and the attachés of the post.

The first Americans who settled in St. Charles County, and in fact, the first Americans who permanently settled in the State of Missouri, were Col. Daniel Boone, the distinguished pioneer from Kentucky, and his family, excepting his two daughters Lavinia and Rebecca, who lived and died in Kentucky. Col. Boone came to Missouri in 1795 when the land was under Spanish government and settled in Darst's Bottom which is now the Femme Osage Township. At that time since the area was under Spanish rule, the Boone Family became citizens of Spain until the Louisiana Purchase in 1803.

We have mentioned the Boone Family because they were the first American settlers. Blanchette posed as the head and front—the standard-bearer of the first era of civilization, and the Boone family as the advanced guard—the pioneers of the second era. They came at two distinct periods: the first in 1769, and the latter in 1795; there being an interval of 26 years between the dates of the first and second settlements, during the Spanish government.

It was not, however, until the Boones came that the settlers dared to isolate himself from the sight of the Spanish flag which floated over the military post at St. Charles City. After 1795 the county began to settle, the first pioneers locating in Darst's Bottom in Femme Osage township, and thence in other townships.

Then the Louisiana Purchase of 1803, approved by President Thomas Jefferson, occurred. After 1803, the population of the Missouri territory expanded greatly.

This land was a new opportunity to many Americans from the South and East who served in the Revolutionary War, the War of 1812, the Indian Wars and the Mexican American War. If you participated in one of those wars, you could apply for land in the Louisiana Territory under the U.S. Bounty Land Warrant Program through 1855. In addition, the earthquakes in New Madrid in 1811 and 1812 resulted in the citizens of that area being displaced. In 1815, this also led to the first disaster relief program in the United States, as displaced citizens could claim land elsewhere available through the U.S. Bounty Land Warrant Program.

German immigration into the Missouri Territory began in the late 1820s, when Gottfried Duden came to the United States and studied our country.

> He spent nearly a year in St. Charles, Warren and Montgomery counties traveling under the guidance of Daniel M. Boone, son of Daniel Boone, and others. Duden published a book in Germany regarding this area. The book became extremely popular and "made Duden wealthy." The Germans brought money, bought land, introduced the mechanical arts of the old country, and manufactured many new useful articles. They were known as very honest, industrious, and thrifty people. It is claimed that "no other race of people did more for the development of a country."

Also, during the 1800s, many people traveled through St. Charles County on their roads, specifically the Boone's Lick Road, to get to another nearby Missouri city (Franklin in central Missouri and Independence in western Missouri) or to start a western or southwestern journey on one of the famous trails that were established over the years. These trails were the Santa Fe, the Oregon and the California Gold Rush.

Therefore, during the 1800s and early 1900s, St. Charles County, along with nearby areas in Missouri, became a popular growth area for Americans from the South and East, because of the 1803 Louisiana Purchase and the U.S. Bounty Land Warrants Program; immigrants from Germany and other European countries, enticed by the available land and freedoms that they didn't have before (such as voting and buying and owning land); and people who came through the area on their way to the Santa Fe, the Oregon or the California Gold Rush trails.

"During the 1800s, every municipal and congressional township and every habitable nook and corner of the St. Charles County contained a

Top: Conestoga wagon and ox draft team, typical of those used for travel during the 1800s. *Courtesy of National Park Service, Asset ID 6eaa112204da4bae91a5311d16b84cf9.*

Bottom: A Connecticut family on their way to California passing through St. Charles, May 20, 1922. *John J. Buse Collection (S1083_767), the State Historical Society of Missouri Research Center-Columbia.*

cabin." You might wonder what brought people to the area, and the answers are the land, new freedoms and their desire for a better life.

To familiarize the reader with St. Charles County in the year 1875, a map of western St. Charles County is shown on the following pages. This map was made to the best of our knowledge at the present time. It is similar to a map obtained and used by Gerry Matlock for an article he wrote titled "History of West St. Charles" in the *Messenger-Tribune*, October 19, 1977. This map consists of Cuivre, Callaway, Femme Osage, Dardenne, St. Charles and Portage des Sioux townships. Each township had its towns and villages. All towns, post offices, forts and train stations that existed at that time are approximately located on the map for perspective. Today, some have been abandoned due to changes in roads, railroads, rivers and boundaries; some were absorbed by government projects; and a few names have been changed.

Mills

In the early days, there were no roads, no bridges, no ferry boats and scarcely any conveniences for traveling. Supplies were obtained from St. Louis and transported by horses and wagons on dirt paths which later became dirt roads.

The first mill built in the county in 1801 was Jonathan Bryan's mill located on a branch that emptied into the Femme Osage Creek. This mill only ground corn and was a frame one story building with a capacity of 6 to 10 bushels a day.

Other early water mills were Rutger's, Cottle's, Coontz's, Denny's, and Hoffman's (located on Dardenne Creek), Baldrige's, Zumwalt's, Audrian's and Mollitor's (on Peruque Creek), Dibbit's, Hay's and Taylor's (on the Femme Osage Creek), and McSpaddin's on Callaway's Fork.

[Early horse mills were located on the] residence of Francis Howell, William Crowe, Peter Hoffman, Issac Fulkerson, Jonathan Bryan, and John Pittman. The first gun powder mill was built on Howell's Prairie by P.K. Robbins. Robert Beatty built a mill in Green's Bottom. McSpaddin operated one near the Little Femme Osage. Francis Howell made gun powder by hand and sold it for $1 a pound.

MAP OF WESTERN ST. CHARLES

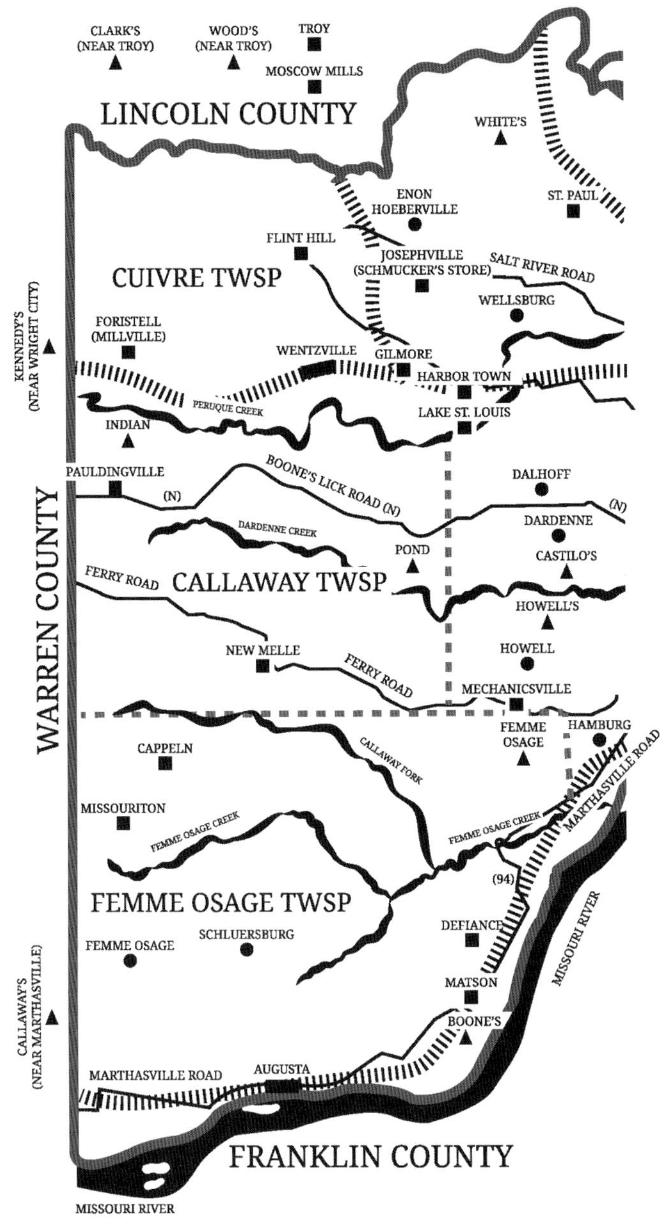

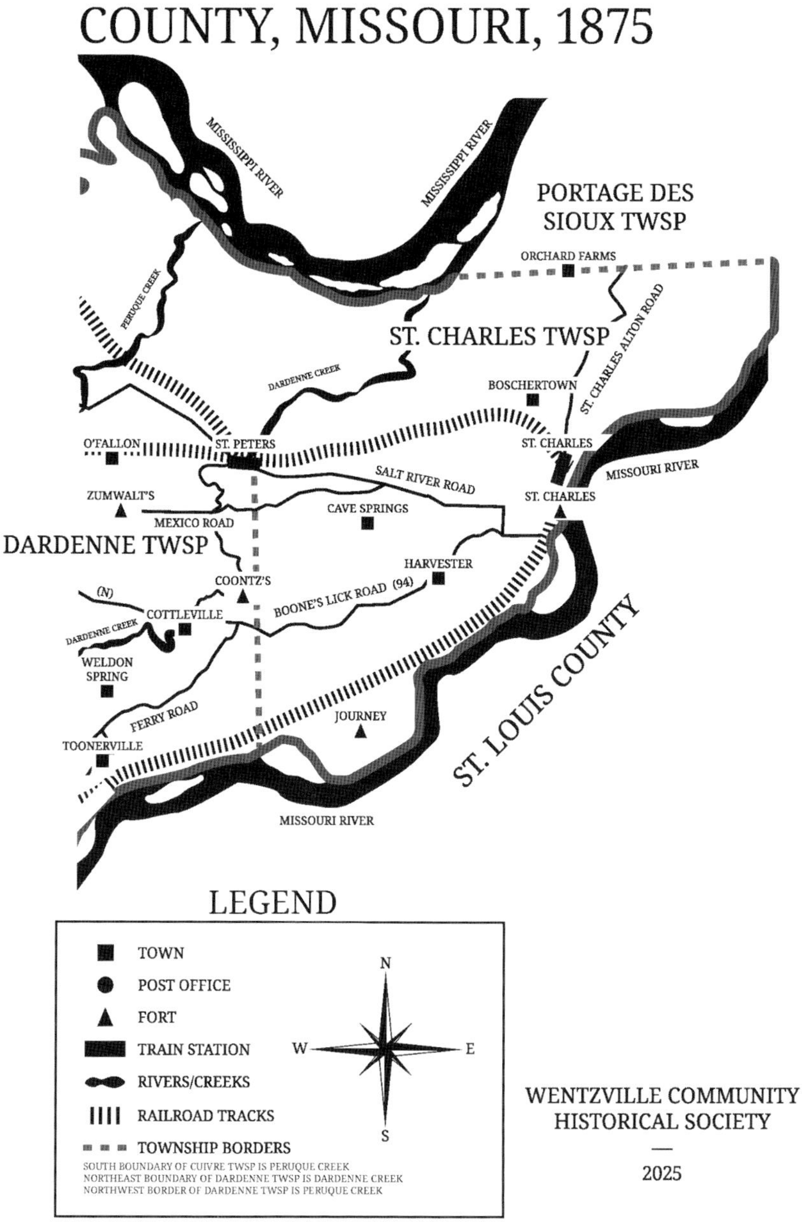

Map of western St. Charles County, Missouri, 1875. *Wentzville Community Historical Society (WCHS) Collection.*

Forts

Several forts were built in the county, and from time to time, several companies of rangers were formed for defensive and offensive operations.

> The principal fort was Daniel M. Boone's (son of Daniel Boone) in Darst's Bottom, which was the largest and strongest. Other forts were Howell's on Howell's Prairie, Pond's Fort on the Dardenne Prairie just south of Wentzville, White's Fort on Dog Prairie near St. Paul, Coontz's on the Boone's Lick Road eight miles west of St. Charles, Zumwalt's at O'Fallon, and Castlio's near Howell's Prairie. Journey Fort was in the south-eastern portion of the county and Indian Fort was located near Foristell.

The image below is of Pond Fort Inn on Boone's Lick Road, where travelers in covered wagons and stagecoaches stopped overnight. The inn was built from logs from the 1812 Pond Fort on Spanish Grant 931 belonging to J. and Malachi Baldridge. The inn was built by Robert Bailey around 1819. Logs from torn-down forts and other buildings were often reused for other buildings, so as not to waste natural resources.

"In Warren County, Kennedy's Fort was built near Wright City and Callaway's Fort near Marthasville. In Lincoln County near Troy were located Clark's Fort and Wood's Fort."

Pond Fort Inn on Boone's Lick Road was built in 1819 using logs from the 1812 Pond Fort on Spanish Grant 931 belonging to J. and Malachi Baldridge. *WCHS Collection.*

County Roads

By 1885, many roads had been established—not roads as we think of them today but narrow dirt roads.

> Principal roads at this time were Boone's Lick Road (26 miles), Salt River Road (28 miles), Mexico Road (24 miles), Marthasville Road (40 miles), Ferry Road (13 miles), and St. Charles Alton Road (22 miles). Other roads, not located on the map are: Howell's Ferry Road that commenced at Flint Hill connecting with Salt River Road and running south easterly crossing Mexico Road, Peruque Creek, Boone's Lick Road, Dardenne Creek, Marthasville Road to the Missouri River at Howell's Ferry and the St. Charles Road, running from New Melle southwest to Femme Osage Post Office, terminating at Augusta.

Pioneers

The tables on the following pages list the names of the pioneers of four townships in western St. Charles County along with the official number and acreage of their land grants. There are three "arps" identified in the Cuivre township. *Arp* stands for *arpent*, an old Canadian French word. An arp is equivalent to .84 acres.

It is known that the Spanish land grants were randomly situated and were not laid out east-west and north-south. If you ever see a map of early 1800s Spanish land grants, you'll notice that Spanish land grants were seldom square.

The data for tables 1–4 comes from the book *History of St. Charles, Montgomery and Warren Counties, pages 101–03.*

TABLE 1. PIONEERS OF CALLAWAY TOWNSHIP

	Grant No.	Acres		Grant No.	Acres
David Baldridge	738	640	J. Baldridge	931	340
Robert Baldridge	1,807	640	M. Baldridge	297	640
William Crow	891	640	Leonard Price	61	552
Andrew Edwards	738	640	John Parett		552
David Edwards	1,807	640	Arend Rutgers	1,669	5,908
David Kichlie	947	640	P. Zumwalt	53	300
David Kichlie	418	510			

TABLE 2. PIONEERS OF CUIVRE TOWNSHIP

	Grant No.	Acres		Grant No.	Acres
J. Baker	2,573	212	Silvanus Cottle	756	(arp) 500
David Conrad	1,783	640	G. Fallis	456	350
Bernard Praft and J. Beauchemin		1,361	Wm. Farnsworth	754	640
			August Giles	888	640
Jacob Cottle	755	640	Benjamin Jones	935	640
Lewis Crow	1,777	640	A Keithley	1,781	(arp) 300
William Craig	889	640	S. Lewis	1,782	640
M. Lewis	929	552	J. Wealthy	11	340
C.A. Macay	8	429	H. Zumwalt	413	737
Redenhour McCrow	140	...	Ad. Zumwalt	294	510
Fr. Hostetter	...	425	C. Zumwalt	54	167
Daniel McCoy	386	300	J. Zumwalt	287	(arp) 350
John McCoy	145	382			

Arp stands for *arpent*, a Canadian or old French word. An arp is equivalent to .84 acres.

Table 3. Pioneers of Dardenne Township

	Grant No.	Acres		Grant No.	Acres
Perry Brown	296	493	Milton Lewis	1,771	299
J. Beatty	991	640	David Miracle	168	340
Warren Cottle	354 753	640	William McConnel	292	680
Coontz	739	640	John McConnel	1,785	640
Ira Cottle	353	340	John Rourke	3,225 260	640
Nich. Coontz	58	340	Rutgers	1,669	5,908
P. Chouteau	1,704	433	Na. Simmonds	1,776	255
Grojean	460	170	John Scott	1,690	428
Francis Howell	887	640	Joseph St. Mary	2,526	160
George Hoffman	293	340	John A. Smith	735	640
P. Hoffman	57	255	Teaque	174	640
George Hoffman	1,787	640	Joseph Weldon	280	340
John Howell	453	344	John Weldon	1,796	425
Newton Howell	---	279	Christ Wolf	948	640
James Kerr	1,641	1,020	John Walker	67	340
Godfrey Krah	424	510	Joseph Voisard	1,786	640
George Gatty	290	382	Ad. Zumwalt	296	493

Table 4. Pioneers of Femme Osage

	Grant No.	Acres		Grant No.	Acres
John Bell	1,721	382	John Little Johns	1,792	640
Daniel Boone	1,646	450	S. Hammond	476	825
Daniel M. Boone	20	510	Joseph Haynes	14	170
Nathan Boone	1,794	680	John Lindsay	59	425
G. Buchanan	1,722	340	William Hays	1,670	510

	Grant No.	Acres		Grant No.	Acres
Jonathan Bryan	301	527	H. McLaughlin	44	510
James Clay	138	279	McCourtney	475	340
Jeremiah Clay	300	382	J. McMitchell	384	595
John Crow	438	382	Adam Martin	1,673	510
Henry Crow	62	340	Thomas Smith	303	680
David Darst Sr.	18	510	Perceley's Representative	937	640
David Darst	1,643	224	John Watkins	1,735	680
James Davis	970	340	Isaac Van Bibber	19	340
Joshua Dodson	208	340	James Van Bibber	1,793	362
Isa Darst	1,644	297	John Zumwalt	1,246	640

EXPERIENCES OF THE EARLY PIONEERS

By Gerry Matlock
Originally published in the Wentzville Union, *May 7, 1975*

In the 1885 book *History of St. Charles, Montgomery and Warren Counties, Missouri* (mentioned at the beginning of chapter 1), the experiences of the early pioneers are described as follows:

> [The early settlers had] their privations and hardships, but they also had their own peculiar joys. If they were poor, they were free also from the anxiety and care that always attends the possession of wealth.
>
> If they had few neighbors, they were on the best of terms with those they had. A common interest and a common sympathy bound them together with the strongest ties. They were a little world to themselves, and the good feeling that prevailed was all the stronger because they were so far removed from the great world of the East.
>
> Among these pioneers there was realized such a community of interest that there existed a community of feeling. They were bound together with such a strong bond of sympathy, inspired by the consciousness of common hardship. Neighbors did not

Three pioneers visiting outside. They may be talking about a hunting trip or what meat they need for the winter. *WCHS Collection.*

even wait for an invitation or request to help one another. Was a settler's cabin burned or blown down? No sooner was the fact known throughout the neighborhood than the settlers assembled to assist the unfortunate one to rebuild his home. They came with as little hesitation, and with as much alacrity, as though they were all members of the same family and bound together by ties of blood. One man's interest was every other man's interest.

There was no danger of being ordered off a man's premises or arrested for trespassing. One of the peculiar circumstances that surrounded the early life of the pioneers was a strange loneliness. The solitude seemed almost to oppress them. Months would pass during which they would scarcely see a human face outside their own families.

On occasions of special interest, such as elections, holiday celebrations, or camp-religious meetings, it was nothing unusual for a few settlers who lived in the immediate neighborhood of the meeting to entertain scores of those who had come from a distance.

> Rough and rude though the surroundings may have been, the pioneers were none the less honest, sincere, hospitable, and kind in their relations. It is true, as a rule, and of universal application, that there is a greater degree of real humanity among the pioneers of any country than there is when the country becomes old and rich.

In contrasting the present social affairs with pioneer times, one has well said,

> Then, if a house was to be raised, every man "turned out," and often the women, too, and while the men piled up the logs that fashioned the primitive dwelling place, the women prepared the dinner.
>
> Sometimes it was cooked by big log fires near the site where the cabin was building; in other cases, it was prepared at the nearest cabin, and at the proper hour was carried to where the men were at work. If one man in the neighborhood killed a beef, a pig or a deer, every other family in the neighborhood was sure to receive a piece.
>
> We were all on an equality. Aristocratic feelings were unknown and would not have been tolerated. What one had we all had. But today if you lean against a neighbor's shade tree, he will charge you for it. If you are poor and fall sick you may lie and suffer almost unnoticed and unattended, and probably go to the poorhouse; and just as like as not the man who would report you to the authorities as a subject of county care would charge the county for making the report.
>
> It was common thing in the early times for hardened men, who had no fears of jails or penitentiaries, to stand in great fear of the indignation of a pioneer community. Such was some of the characteristics of St. Charles County.
>
> This general state of feeling among the pioneers was by no means peculiar to St. Charles County, although it was strongly illustrated here. It prevailed generally throughout the West during the time of the early settlement. The very nature of things taught the settlers the necessity of dwelling together in this spirit. It was their only protection.
>
> They had come far away from the well-established reign of law, and entered a new country, where civil authority was totally unable to afford protection and redress grievances. Here the settlers lived some time before there was an officer of the law in the county. Each man's protection was in the goodwill and friendship of those about

> him, and the thing that any man might well dread was the ill will of the community. It was more terrible than the law.
>
> Music of the natural order was not wanting, and every night the pioneers were lulled to rest by the screeching of panthers and the howling of wolves. When the dogs ventured too far out from the cabins at night, they would be driven back by the wolves chasing them up to the very cabin doors. Trapping wolves became a very profitable business after the State began to pay a bounty for wolf scalps.

While the above description of early settler life is romanticized, it no doubt has some basis in truth.

Food

> In addition to ground corn provided by the mills or hominy-blocks, meat was plentiful. Deer could be seen daily in droves of from 12 to 20, and sometimes as many as 50 would be seen grazing together. Elk were also found, and wild turkeys and prairie chickens without number. Bears were not unknown. All the streams of water also abounded in fish. Sometimes large parties would get together, and, having been provided with cooking utensils and facilities for camping out, would go off some distance and spend weeks together. In fact, game was so plentiful in the early years that the early pioneers could not envision a time when game would be scarce.

House and Home Comforts

The first buildings in the county were not just like the log cabins that immediately succeeded them. The latter required some help and a great deal of labor to build.

> The very first buildings constructed were a cross between "hoop cabins" and Indian bark huts.
>
> As soon as enough men could get together for a "cabin raising" then log cabins were in style. Many a pioneer remembered the

Top: The original Curtis Cannon log cabin built in 1811 on Big Creek, five miles north of Foristell. This picture is dated 1923; the cabin no longer exists. *WCHS Collection.*

Bottom: The original log cabin of Daniel Boone at Femme Osage, Missouri. *John Buse Collection, Identifier S1083_741; SHSMO-Columbia.*

Families in 1812 lived in log cabins like this one, which stands on Point Prairie Road, Wentzville. They fled to the nearest fort when there was an Indian scare. *WCHS Collection.*

happiest time of their life, as that when they lived in one of these homely but comfortable old cabins.

A window with sash and glass was a rarity and was evidence of wealth and aristocracy which but few could support. They were often made with greased paper put over the window, which admitted a little light, but more often there was nothing whatever over it, or the cracks between the logs, without either chinking or daubing, were the dependence on light and air.

The doors were fastened with old-fashioned wooden latches, and for a friend, or neighbor, or traveler, the string always hung out, for the pioneers of the West were hospitable and entertained visitors to the best of their ability. It is noticeable with what affection the pioneers speak of their old log cabins.

Top: Old log cabin homestead was at Whitehead and Pitman in Wentzville. It was torn down in 1930. *WCHS Collection.*

Bottom: Fort Zumwalt log cabin built in the late 1800s. A replica of the fort was built in the 2010s and is now open for summer tours. *John Buse Collection, Identifier S1083_1625; SHSMO-Columbia.*

The people of today, familiar with cooking stoves, ranges, refrigerators, microwaves, slow cookers, air fryers and so forth would most likely be lost if they were compelled to prepare a meal with no other conveniences than those provided in a pioneer cabin.

> Rude fireplaces were built in chimneys composed of mud and sticks, or, at best, undressed stone. These fireplaces served for heating and cooking purposes; also, for ventilation. Around the cheerful blaze of this fire the meal was prepared.

Railroads and National Roadways

By Lois Kessler, August 2024

Starting in 1855 and onward, the facilities for the transportation of produce to market in St. Charles County were unsurpassed by those in any other county in the state.* There was a good market at St. Charles, St. Louis and Alton for most of the farm products. There were the Missouri and Mississippi Rivers hugging this territory more than halfway around it, with ten shipping points on the Missouri and eleven on the Mississippi. But especially important was the beginning of the railroad. The earliest railroad nearby was the Missouri Cross Railroad, which connected several towns in Illinois in the late 1830s, St. Charles being one hundred miles away. This caused no interest in Missouri. Missourians in the early to mid-1800s were convinced that their progress and growth were closely allied with river transportation.

Up until the mid- to late 1800s, steamboats were widely used at St. Charles City for transportation of products and people. Visionaries like William Allen, the founder of Wentzville, saw that the railroad would not only aid in the transportation of goods and people but would also be instrumental in the development of the land in the interior of the county and state.

According to the Wabash Railroad Historical Society, in 1851, a group of pioneer railroad men secured a charter from the State of Missouri for

---

* A large portion of the information in this section comes from the article titled "About the Wabash Railroad" published by the Wabash Railroad Historical Society on its website in July 2024: www.wabashrhs.org/p/wabash-railroad.html.

The steamboat *Louisiana* at the St. Charles riverfront. *John Buse Collection, Identifier S1083_1724; SHSMO-Columbia.*

building the North Missouri Railroad connecting St. Louis to the Missouri-Iowa border. This railroad was planned to connect to other railroads/cities in three phases. The first phase was to connect St. Louis to East St. Charles. Construction started in 1854, and the line opened on August 20, 1855.

This is when William Allen entered the picture. Allen contacted his neighbors, and after talking it through, they realized that if a railroad line could be added connecting St. Charles to their area and continuing west, this would add a valuable means of transport for their agriculture goods. In addition, the railroad could create new growth and businesses for their area or village. Allen and his neighbors agreed to donate land for a railroad line through their new village to St. Charles. The land donated had a "wide right of way for lumberyards, grain elevators and other facilities that needed direct rail access." Allen worked with E.L. Wentz, chief engineer of the North Missouri Railroad, to get approval from the North Missouri Railroad and the State of Missouri to add the new village and other stops west of it to the line. It was approved by North Missouri Railroad's Board and by the State of Missouri and the first train arrived in Wentzville in 1857. This new village was named Wentzville in honor of E.L. Wentz. William Allen also

The Wentzville train station surrounded by men and women waiting for their train. *Courtesy of St. Charles County Historical Society.*

paid for the railroad station to be built in the new town of Wentzville, and he became the first station agent at Wentzville.

The North Missouri Railroad continued with second and third phases to extend its lines from St. Charles to Hudson, Missouri (modern-day Macon), which would connect to the Hannibal and St. Joseph Railroad. The second phase started in 1855 and opened on February 1, 1858. The third phase was to connect Hudson, Missouri, to the Missouri-Iowa border, but the Civil War started in 1861 and it placed a hold on the third phase.

But there was still a problem with a railroad connection from St. Charles to St. Louis: there was no bridge over the Missouri River connecting St. Charles to St. Louis.

> Until 1864...it was necessary to unload all freight and passengers on the east bank of the river at St. Charles, ferry the people and the goods across, and reload on the opposite side. In 1864, a car ferry arrangement was effected eliminated the necessity for this unload and reloading the cars.

Throughout the 1800s, established ferries transferred people over the Missouri River between St. Charles and St. Louis County. Then the Civil War started, and the North Missouri Railroad and other railroads were used to easily and quickly transport goods and men from one location to another.

Top: The North Missouri Railroad ferry that transferred railroad cars across the Missouri River from St. Charles to St. Louis. *John J. Buse Collection (S1083_122); SHSMO-Columbia.*

Bottom: The John L. Ferguson Steamboat Ferry was used to transfer people across the Missouri River from 1860 to 1930. *John J. Buse Collection (S1083_1726); SHSMO-Columbia.*

The North Missouri Railroad's property was a military objective for both the Union and Confederate Armies operating nearby in the years from 1861 to 1865. Captain "Bloody Bill" Anderson of the Confederate and a small group of men destroyed railroad tracks, stations, bridges, culverts and cars; tore up rails; and destroyed and burned fuel supplies in the St. Charles County area throughout the Civil War. In 1864, more than 120 men who tried to stop the Confederate invaders were killed, and many of them are buried along the right-of-way near Centralia in Boone County.

The image below shows a Union blockhouse at the Peruque Bridge on North Missouri Railroad near Wentzville. The Peruque Bridge was destroyed during the Civil War.

> Following the [Civil] War, the North Missouri Railroad began to rebuild the lines destroyed in military maneuvers and also began

The Union blockhouse at Peruque Bridge on the North Missouri Railroad. Southern soldiers destroyed and burned bridges, tracks and railroad stations during the Civil War. *Identifier P0170; SHSMO-St. Louis.*

> the construction of what was then known as the "West Branch," a line running from Moberly [Missouri] to Birmingham, a small town near Kansas City. Both the West Branch and the third division of the North Missouri were completed in 1868.

In 1871, according to the Wabash Railroad Historical Society, a bridge across the Missouri River was completed at St. Charles, and the North Missouri Railroad and the predecessors of the Wabash joined to provide a continuous line from Toledo, Ohio, in the east to the western part of Missouri. Less than three months after the bridge was completed, there was a reorganization of the North Missouri Railroad, and as a result of foreclosure action, the entire property became known as the St. Louis, Kansas City and Northern Railroad.

Another merger occurred in 1879. The Wabash Railroad Company (operating east of the Mississippi) and the St. Louis, Kansas City and Northern Railroad (operating west of the Mississippi) were merged into the Wabash, St. Louis and Pacific Railroad Company. At this time, the railroad added passenger-service-only trains, which prompted the addition of hotels and commercial establishments near the train tracks. Until 1855, people traveled by stage, wagon or boat.

Unfortunately, on November 8, 1879, a span of the Missouri River bridge completed in 1871 gave way. Over time, both engines and cars had become heavier, and the bridge was made of cast iron and steel, which could not support their weight. The bridge was rebuilt but collapsed again in 1881; at that time, the cast iron was replaced with wrought iron. The new steel structure bridge was used until 1931, when it was replaced by the present "Pitcairn" bridge used by the Wabash Railroad Company.

As for highway bridges, construction of the first highway bridge over the Missouri River (connecting St. Charles and St. Louis County) started in 1902 and was completed in 1904. The impending world's fair in St. Louis added to citizens' impatience for the completion of the new bridge. An agreement was made between the bridge company and the railroad: the railroad would operate trolley cars over the bridge for fifty years at a toll of five cents per passenger plus 10 percent of gross receipts.

> Before 1885, United States engineers, in locating the great National Turnpike, the first major improved highway in the country built by the federal government, understood that St. Charles was fast becoming a central point for the transfer of goods and people. The U.S. engineers

Railroad locomotives with only passenger cars were added by the Wabash Railroad in 1879. *WCHS Collection.*

> determined that from Maryland, the cheapest and most direct route through the States pointed directly to the northern shores of the Missouri River, via St. Charles, to Jefferson City. In other words, the north side of the river was more conducive to construction for a cheaper cost because of the topography of the land.

This happened because St. Charles lay right in the line of the national highway of travel (the roads being built from the East to the West across the United States), and the topographical configuration of the country placed it there. South of the Missouri River is a broken, jagged, mountainous region, unfit at the time for cheap, direct lines of transportation, while north of the river, roads could be run through the country at will without encountering any permanent obstacle.

Thus, highway and interstate traffic began when more and more people began to use automobiles, and the "Crossroads of Nation" moniker was developed in Wentzville, referring to the intersection of US Highways 40 and 61.

Chapter 2

The Beginning of Wentzville in 1855 and the Civil War in Wentzville

By Lois Kessler, Gerry Matlock and Kathy Weindel

William Milton Allen, Founder of Wentzville

By Gerald Matlock
Originally published in the Wentzville Union*, May 14, 1975*
Additional information added by Lois Kessler, August 2024

Author's note: Large sections of Matlock's original article were taken directly from the book *History of St. Charles, Montgomery and Warren Counties, Missouri*, originally published in 1885 and now in the public domain.

William Milton Allen was the son of Reverend Joseph Smith Allen (1779–1834) and Rachel McFarland May (1792–1840). Joseph and Rachel were Virginia natives and married in 1811 just across the Virginia state line in Rockingham County, North Carolina.

William Milton Allen, the subject of the present sketch, was born of this union in Henry County, Virginia, on September 3, 1812. The family came to Missouri in 1829 when William was about seventeen years of age and settled in the Flint Hill area. His father was a minister of the M.E. Church and a successful farmer. After his father's death, William continued to farm. As an early settler of the area, he was a large landholder, and as a representative of an old and well-known Virginia family, he was also a slaveholder. He was considered a man of easy circumstances with a good education and was thought to have always "shown a marked taste of mental culture."

Later, he became interested in merchandising and soon became one of the substantial citizens of the county. It has been noted that Allen always showed commendable public spirit for the advancement of the general interests of St. Charles County and particularly the Wentzville area.

On November 1, 1833, Allen married Mary "Polly" A. Miller Shelton (1811–1861), a daughter of James C. Shelton of St. Charles County but, like, the Allens formerly of Virginia. Together they had eight children. All but the youngest daughter are buried in Linn Cemetery in Wentzville.

1. Elizabeth F. (1834–1860), m. George Smith Myers (1832–1910)
2. Rachel Ann (1836–1914), m. Thomas Carr Boyd (1821–1899)
3. Joseph J. (1838–1849)
4. Tabitha Susan (1840–1920), m. Joseph Smith Allen (1840–1895)
5. Mary Milton (1842–1897), m. Warren W. Walker (1838–1920)
6. William S. (1845–1846)
7. William Headly (1847–1923), m. Emma Simms (1854–1937)
8. Nancy "Nannie" M. (1850–1932), m. Thomas F. Riddle (1842–1880)

Wentzville's Founder

Around the 1850s, the North Missouri Railroad was pushing across Missouri to the west to furnish services for residents of Missouri and to make it easier for the farmers to send their products to market. In the Wentzville area, the major crop was tobacco. William M. Allen donated land and money for the building of the tracks and persuaded other farmers to donate land and money for the same purpose.

Neighbors of Mr. Allen were Mr. and Mrs. C.H. Wentz, who came from New York. Mr. Wentz was employed by the railroad. There was no town here, which was required in order that the railroad would stop. Therefore, Allen, assisted by Wentz, planned a town in 1855, which consisted of a narrow tract of land about seven blocks long. They conducted their survey and had the plat duly recorded according to the requirements of the law. (It should be noted that, since this article was first published, further research has indicated that it was Mr. Wentz's uncle Erasmus L. Wentz who helped

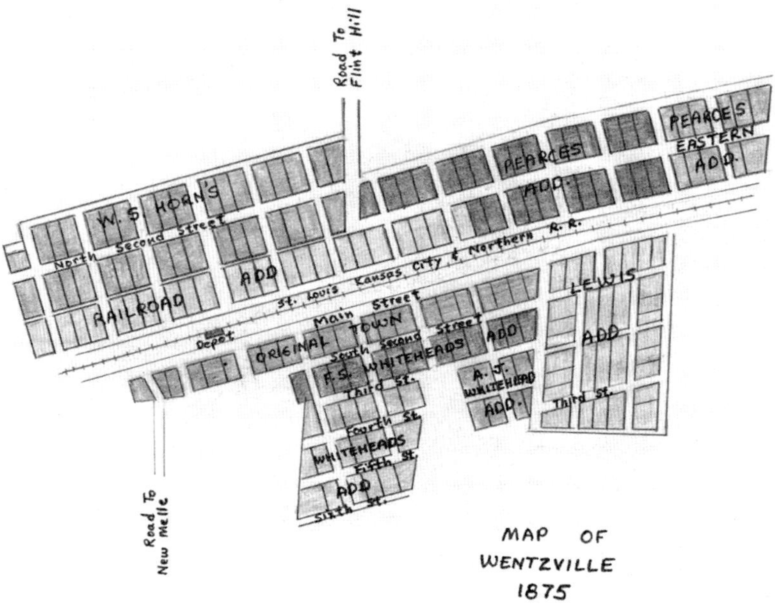

Mr. Allen. In an interview conducted by Mary McEhliney of St. Charles before his death, Mr. Allen said he did not remember the man's first name.)

Allen honored Mr. Wentz by naming the town after him. Afterward, Allen built the train depot at Wentzville and accepted the appointment of station agent to get Wentzville established as a regular stopping place or station on the road. The original train station in Wentzville was west of South Linn Avenue, on the north side of West Main Street. In the 1940s, as men were returning home from World War II, the station was moved to east of South Linn Avenue. It stood about where the train caboose is as of 2024. The original deed indicated that if the station ceased to exist, the ground would be returned to the Allen family. Today, the ground is considered railroad right-of-way, but research at this time has not indicated how or when that came about.

In addition to the train station, Mr. Allen built the first house and store erected in Wentzville. In 1856, he built a large home in the area now bounded by Pitman Avenue and Luetkenhaus Boulevard. In the McEhliney interview referenced earlier, Mr. Allen is quoted as saying, "I like to be pretentious" and "My wife was socially inclined, liked parties, and often planned gala festivities." In 1863, just seven years after building the home, Allen sold the property to Lawrence and Elizabeth Garey Matthews (their name is often

Opposite: Wentzville's 1875 plat map. *WCHS Collection.*

Right: William M. Allen's home, built in 1855–56. *WCHS Collection.*

spelled with one *t*). It's not clear what prompted Allen to sell the home: maybe the death of his wife in 1861 or losses from the Civil War. The home would eventually become known as the Gannaway home. In 1857, William Allen built the first store and established Allen, Whitehead & Co. That building still stands on the southeast corner of East Main Street and South Linn Avenue.

The Politician

William Allen was a highly respected man who became well known as "public spirited and influential in Western St. Charles County." The following paragraphs are from a book written in 1886 and illustrate the population's opinion of him:

> Mr. Allen was a prominent man in politics of the county and was originally associated with the Whig party. Mr. Allen was first elected to the Legislature in about 1846, though he had previously been quite active and prominent in county politics. Four years later he was elected to the State Senate. In conjunction with State Senator Reed, of Callaway County, Allen was mainly instrumental in obtaining the charter of the Old North Missouri Railroad.

As a legislator Mr. Allen "proved a sound conservative and faithful representative of the people." He was considered "a man of strong natural ability and good sound judgement." "An industrious and extensive reader, he early became a man of large information, and on account of his character and ability was soon accorded a position among the leaders of his party.

He was an active canvasser in his political life and although a representative of the minority party in the county, he had the happy faculty of putting the questions at issue before the people in such a light as to win for his views and opinions their hearty endorsement. One illustration of this will suffice: The Democrats were unanimously opposed to internal improvements by the general government. But Congress had passed an act making an appropriation for and authorizing the building of a national turnpike from the Atlantic seaboard westward through the different state capitals along the general route of the road. As this would have to come to Jefferson City, it could not fail to pass through St. Charles County, and of course the great advantages that would thus accrue to the county could be dwelt upon with great fervor and effect. "Democrats though the majority of the people were, the advocacy of this particular road was a winning card, and Mr. Allen had the tact to see this and to address it for all it was worth."

Civil War

William Allen was a southerner at heart and supported the Confederacy during the Civil War. In 1860 according to the slave schedule, he enslaved twenty-eight people, of which half were under the age of twelve. In 1861, he was taken prisoner by Union troops and held prisoner of war in the St. Louis Arsenal (date unknown), to be freed after taking a loyalty oath to the Union. While Allen being taken prisoner is widely reported in various sources, to date, we have been unable to find any official records.

Final Years

William Allen's final years were spent living with a daughter and, later, a son in Wentzville. He died on May 6, 1892, and is buried with members of his family in Linn Cemetery, Wentzville. Sadly, the historical society has not been able to find a photograph of Mr. Allen.

Erasmus Livingston Wentz

By Kathy Weindel, August 2024

Erasmus Livingston Wentz was born in Binghamton, Broome County, New York, in 1818 to William and Sally Wentz. As a child, Wentz grew up with five siblings. When his mother died in 1835, his father remarried and had eight more children, and Wentz became the eldest brother to twelve siblings. Since Wentz's father, William, was a teacher, it is probable that he educated Wentz and his siblings. In addition to being a teacher, Wentz's father was a self-taught civil engineer. Wentz followed in his father's footsteps and became a civil engineer. He did not have a formal education, and he did not attend engineering school. Instead, he gained his skills and knowledge of engineering from his father and from working on canal and railroad construction projects during the 1830s and '40s.

Wentz began his career as a civil engineer at the age of sixteen, as an axe man on a survey crew for the Erie railroad. The axe man would clear branches and brush for the survey team to offer a clear line of sight for the surveyor and also notch trees to indicate border lines. By 1836, he had been promoted to the position of assistant engineer. Between 1837 and 1839, he was a principal assistant engineer for the Saginaw and Grand River Canal project in Michigan. From 1840 until early 1853, Wentz was a supervising engineer on the Susquehanna Division of the Erie Railroad Line.

In 1853, Wentz accepted a position on the North Missouri Railroad as a civil engineer. Two years prior, in March 1851, the North Missouri Railroad Company had been granted a charter from the Missouri General Assembly to build a railway line in northern Missouri along the dividing ridge between the Missouri River to the south and the Mississippi River to the east. The railway line route would eventually lie between St. Charles, Missouri, and the southern border of Iowa. In 1852, the charter was amended to extend the route to St. Louis, Missouri.

Before work could begin on the construction of the railroad, surveys had to be done to determine the best route. As Wentz had skills in and knowledge of surveying and mapping, it is probable that he was assigned to lead a survey crew into northern Missouri in search of the best possible route. And the best possible route was one that required the least amount of grading and the fewest trestles to build and was sparsely populated. In 1854, on completion of the surveys, a report was presented to the board of directors with a recommendation of the most favorable route. The board of directors approved the selected route, and within the year, construction began.

Construction of the railroad was done in sections or divisions: the first section was from St. Louis to the eastern bank of the Missouri River, while the second division was from St. Charles to Hudson (Macon, Missouri), and the third section would proceed from Hudson (modern-day Macon) to the southern border of Iowa.

Each division was supervised by a division engineer who had the authority and power to make decisions regarding his division, including the acquisition of land. By 1855, Wentz held the position of division engineer of the eastern division and oversaw railroad construction of the second section from St. Charles to Hudson (modern-day Macon).

Unlike large railroad companies that were given large tracts of land from the federal government during the 1800s, small railroad companies such as the North Missouri were not as fortunate and would often have to purchase land from landowners or farmers. However, there were those landowners who were willing to give land in exchange for concessions made by the railroad companies. One such landowner was William M. Allen.

By 1855, track had been laid east of the small community (village) that Allen had established. Allen realized that the railroad company as well as his community could benefit from tracks being built on his and his neighbors' lands.

Allen approached Wentz with an offer. Allen and his neighbors would give a portion of their lands as a right-of-way to the railroad company, and in exchange, the railroad company would lay track on the donated property. In addition, Allen negotiated for a depot and to be appointed depot stationmaster. It is likely that Wentz accepted Allen's offer because it would save the North Missouri Railroad Company the expense of purchasing privately owned lands.

In recognition of Wentz's acceptance of the offer and his surveying of town land plats, Allen, with the approval of his neighbors, named their small community in honor of Wentz. So in late 1855, Allen's small village,

The Wabash train station in Wentzville that William Allen built in 1855, pictured here in 1915. *WCHS Collection.*

with a depot and a railroad line running through it, came to be known as Wentzville.

Within the year, Wentz resigned from his position with the North Missouri Railroad, but he did continue working as a civil engineer. Between 1857 and 1858, while Wentz was still living in St. Charles, Missouri, he took the position of construction engineer for the Chicago and Alton Railroad. In late 1858, he left Missouri and moved to Texas, where he became chief engineer for the Texas and New Orleans Railroad. Wentz left Texas in 1859 and returned to Binghamton, New York, where he continued working as a civil engineer, surveying land and mapping until the outbreak of the Civil War.

When the Civil War began in 1861, Wentz enlisted in the Union army with the rank of major. By 1862, Wentz was a military engineer with the U.S. Military Railroads of Virginia. That year, Wentz was promoted to chief engineer and general superintendent on the Norfolk and Petersburg Railroad in Virginia, and by 1863, he held the position of superintendent and engineer. In 1864, he was promoted to chief engineer and general superintendent in charge of the operations of the military railroad system in Virginia.

After the Civil War ended in 1865, Wentz stayed in Virginia and tried his hand at farming and working as a land surveyor for a few years.

By the mid-1870s, Wentz had returned to Missouri, where he found employment with the Atlantic and Pacific Railroad Company until 1877. During his time with the railroad, Wentz served as an assistant superintendent and then became a division superintendent in 1876. But by the early part of 1877, he had ended his association with the Atlantic and Pacific Railroad.

In the spring of 1877, Wentz found employment with the Missouri and Pacific Railroad; he held the positions of fuel agent and supply agent. For a period, he was manager of the engineering office located at the company's headquarters in St. Louis, Missouri. By 1881, Wentz had been promoted to resident engineer, and he was placed in charge of overseeing railroad construction through Missouri, Kansas and the Indian Territory (Oklahoma). Wentz continued to work for the railroad until the late 1880s.

During this time, Wentz was also engaged by the Laclede and Creve Coeur Railroad Company as a construction engineer to supervise building a short line from St. Louis to the Creve Coeur lakes located in the western part of the St. Louis County. The line was used to transport tourists to the lakes.

Amid concerns about his health, Wentz retired from the Missouri Pacific Railroad Company, and by the early 1890s, he had moved to Michigan, where he lived near his sister and her family. For a few years, he had a small civil engineering company, doing land surveying and mapping for individuals and the community of Bay City, Michigan, where he lived until his death in 1899. Although Wentz died in Michigan, his body was taken to Binghamton, New York, where he was buried alongside his parents, William and Sally Wentz.

Civil War Skirmish in Wentzville, July 15–16, 1861

By Gerry Matlock
Originally published in the Wentzville Union*, October 22, 1975*
Additional research by Lois Kessler, August 2024

Information regarding the effect of the Civil War on our community is somewhat scarce. This lack of detailed information reflects the divided views of the people and the tendency of people not to discuss the issue, which would bring up hard feelings. When people did discuss and record the history of the war later, memories had faded, and oftentimes, conflicting records exist.

The history of the event as found in the various literature is presented in this article. The detailed truths may never be decided; however, generalities exist. One thing is certain: over a half million men died in the conflict. There was unbelievable destruction of property, and personal wounds were inflicted that would take generations to heal.

Missouri, being a slave state, was largely identified in interest and sympathy with her sister states of the South. Many of her people, however—undoubtedly, most of them—were opposed to secession, except as a last resort. Until the war began, most the people were in favor of Missouri taking a neutral position. When all hope of compromise failed, a large number favored the Southern cause and either openly identified themselves with it or gave it their warmest sympathy.

The first volunteers from St. Charles County were for the Southern service. They were recruited early in 1861 and were called the Missouri State Guard. A company was recruited and was composed of some of the best men in the country. Richard Overall was made captain, David Schultz first lieutenant and Chap. Luckett second lieutenant.

About half the population of St. Charles County was of German birth or descent. The Germans were friends of liberty and equal rights regardless of race or color. Judge Arnold Krekel was their leader and prepared them to hold St. Charles County to the Union cause. Quickly, a company of home guards for the Union was organized. A regiment of twelve companies was formed containing over 1,300 men. Judge Krekel was elected colonel, and the regiment went into camp near Cottleville. Krekel's (German) Dutch, as they were called, did valuable service for the Union cause by holding St. Charles County and preventing the enlistment of Southern volunteers there.

When it was certain that Missouri would be one of the states wherein battles of the Civil War would be fought, the immense importance of preserving and holding the North Missouri Railroad was realized by the authorities of the federal government. The North Missouri Railroad ran through the heart of St. Charles County. The authorities of the railroad were all loyal, and the secessionists regarded it as the great enemy to the Southern cause, to be assailed whenever practicable and, when troops were passing upon it, to be attacked vigorously and with deadly intent. Time and again threats had been made by the secessionists to destroy the bridges and track. For this reason, federal troops were sent from St. Louis to St. Charles County.

In the middle of June 1861, two months after the firing on Fort Sumter, two companies of Colonel B. Gratz Brown's regiment of Union home guards along with Colonel Kallman's regiment of home guards were sent from St. Louis to St. Charles and vicinity to guard bridges and to control the county. They went on an expedition still farther up the railroad and took complete possession of Wentzville in West St. Charles County. They searched the homes of citizens, seized many guns and took several citizens prisoner. They also found a secession flag hidden away in a hayloft. The prisoners were all released upon taking the oath except for William M. Allen, the railroad agent and founder of Wentzville, and John G. Cook, who had guns in his possession. Allen was a very prominent man and had served in the House of Representatives and State Senate between 1845 and 1855. Allen and Cook were transported to St. Louis for questioning. This is believed to have been the first invasion of this part of the state by federal troops. (The Union Provost Marshals' files have no records of Cook's and Allen's arrests.)

On Sunday evening, July 14, 1861, four companies of the Union's Second Missouri Volunteers and two companies of the Eighth Missouri Infantry left the St. Louis arsenal for Mexico, Missouri, and other points on the North Missouri Railroad.

Before arriving at St. Charles on the afternoon of July 15, they had heard of the secession tendencies of the citizens there, but their reception gave no evidence of this. Cheers greeted them on their arrival, and ladies appeared upon the balconies, at the windows and at the doors to wave welcome to them. Their greeting was the same a few miles up the road.

About six miles west of St. Charles, one of the men was shot and wounded from someone under the cover of the woods. It now became evident that they were entering a section of the state where they were to be treated as enemies. Armed lookouts were now stationed on top of the different cars. Men sat at the open windows with muskets in hand, ready to return the fire of any who might be lying in ambush. A handcar was kept in advance of the train to see that the track was clear.

The soldiers reached Wentzville, where they remained long enough to eat supper. Here one of the men was accidentally shot; the wound afterward resulted in his death. Wentzville was comparatively deserted, maybe as a result of the incident in June, and the majority of those who remained regarded the soldiers more with fear than favor. Rumors were rife that they

Top: Confederate sympathizers were held in detention in St. Charles County or taken to St. Louis City. This picture is dated November 4, 1862. *WCHS Collection.*

Bottom: Four railroad employees check the track with a handcar similar to the one used during the July 14, 1861 Civil War skirmish near Wentzville. *WCHS Collection.*

would be waylaid along the whole line of the railroad. It was desirable that they should that night reach Montgomery City, but it was with reluctance that the colonel gave the orders to advance. It was night when the soldiers again started, dark and rainy, and as the long train rolled slowly on behind the handcar, the prospect was forbidding enough.

Three miles west of Wentzville, the sharp crash of a volley of firearms rang out in the night over the pattering of the rain and the rumbling of the cars. A second's pause, and a line of flashing fire passed from end to end of the train. The whizzing of the minié balls was like a hurricane. Orders to cease firing from the railroad cars and to turn out followed, and speedily about half of the battalion were plunged through the woods in the direction indicated by the firing. No signs of the enemy could be found, and flanked by skirmishers, the train backed up to Wentzville. Three of the soldiers were slightly wounded.

On the next morning, July 16, the train was again put in motion. Before leaving, reports by passengers on the down train were received; the secessionists along the line of county through which the federals had to pass were scouring the county, armed and on horseback, gathering in bands to waylay them. The track was to be torn up, bridge burned, etc. A sharp lookout was kept, and although the handcar had now become a forlorn hope, the fear of the foul play prompted its continuance, and there was no scarcity of volunteers to man it. Quietly, the point of attack on the previous evening was passed, but a little distance beyond, a murderous fire was opened on the handcar, wounding five out of the six men who ran it, one of them mortally.

Again, the skirmishers, a full half of the entire force, turned out; this time, daylight aided them. Through the greater part of the day, the skirmishes flanked the cars. Three other attacks were made during the day, but without harm to the federals. The train gradually progressed up the track. Except for the secession scouts, seen hourly, mostly at a safe distance, the county seemed comparatively deserted. Farms had been left in charge of the women. Millville, now Foristell, seemed wholly deserted. At Wright City, only three persons were seen.

That was the way it was recorded in *The History of St. Charles, Warren and Montgomery Counties, Missouri*, written in 1885, only twenty years after the Civil War.

One cannonball, once in the showcase at the Wentzville Public Library back in the days when there was a Wentzville Public Library, was dug up just west of town. This ball is now on display at the WCHS Museum. Apparently, a crate of cannon balls was lost or discarded, since many balls were found at the same time.

This skirmish date is also mentioned in the book *The Civil War Day by Day*, by W. B. Long (as quoted in *Missouri Sketch Book*, by Clifton Edom).

Another account based on an interview by the late historian Mary McElhiney Olsen, of St. Charles, with Robert Darnell, a local resident, is as follows. Darnell was only six years old when the battle took place, but he claimed in the interview to remember it vividly. About thirty men in all (Union and Confederate) were wounded, and there were seven killed on each side. (The National Parks Service only documents seven killed and one wounded on the Union side and makes no mention of the Southern sympathizers.). All the wounded were taken to what was called a hotel to be cared for. (Research indicates that the Wentzville Hotel and the Thompson Hotel were not built until after the war, so more research needs to be done to determine which building the wounded men were taken to.) The main room of an unknown building was made into a temporary hospital. All the women turned out to help the wounded, regardless of which side they fought for. Darnell remembered big kettles of water being brought in. The women did all they could that night to help the men and cried when one fine young man died that night. The next day, the soldiers were taken away, some as prisoners. The story goes that the very next night, someone set fire to the building or hotel that the wounded were taken to, and it was destroyed. (Please remember that peoples' memories were not always accurate, especially about the aforementioned fire and the hotel burning down. It is known that the Thompson Hotel did not burn down, and Dierker's Wentzville Hotel did not burn down until 1867.)

Another story about the Civil War in Wentzville and the Wentzville Hotel can be found in the 1875 *Plat Book*, which includes a biography of George Dierker. He moved from Femme Osage Township to Wentzville in 1858, where he settled permanently and went into the dry goods business with his brother. They were succeeding when the Civil War broke out. Having been infected by "war fever" and impelled by the military courage of the Germans, he entered the United States service and rushed to the front to risk his life and all he had in the defense of his adopted country. George was born about midway in the Atlantic Ocean, while his parents were on their passage to New Orleans. They took the steamer to St. Charles and settled in Femme Osage Township.

George joined the Forty-Ninth Regiment of Missouri Union Volunteers as a private, but his merit soon caused him to be raised to second and then to first lieutenant, in which rank he served during the remainder of the war. When the war ended in 1865, he returned home and built a very fine frame hotel named the Wentzville Hotel. On New Year's night in 1867, this hotel, in the most unaccountable manner, burned down. The fire was first noticed on the second floor in the Ladies' Parlor, where no lamp had been lit by the family that day. How it caught fire is, therefore, a mystery. Boys might have done it with their firecrackers and skyrockets, but is more probable that the hotel was set on fire intentionally. We may have to do some detective work to determine the actual details of the conflict. There definitely was a skirmish that took place near here about this time, but the dates of the building of the hotel, the skirmish and the burning of the hotel seem to be in conflict.

According to the 1875 St. Charles County Plat Book,

> Mr. Dierker left the army poorer than when he entered it. This does him great credit, when it is remembered that officers in his department had a way of amassing a fortune by stealing cotton, and more especially when the temptation was strengthened by the example of his superiors in command, many of whom, even to the rank of major generals, did not fail to avail themselves.

In 1864, the *St. Joseph Herald* newspaper ran a story regarding Wentzville.

> A band of bushwhackers entered Wentzville last Saturday and held high carnival in that place. They were under the command of Ras. Woods, and he caused all the men in town to draw up in a line and took the vote between Abe Lincoln and Jeff Davis. As might be supposed, everyone voted for Jeff Davis, otherwise, they might have been shot down like dogs. They then made them shout for Jeff Davis, Marmaduke, Price, Shelby, and Bill Anderson, calling the latter "that high souled humanitarian." To show his proficiency with the revolver, Woods amused himself shooting the heads off chickens in a barn yard. Scarce a shot failed. Woods carried eight revolvers, a cavalry saber, and a bowie knife. The accoutrements of his men were but little inferior.

An article in the *St. Charles Weekly Cosmos-Monitor* dated June 15, 1881, reported that in Wentzville,

> Everything prospered until the breaking out of the [Civil War]. Wentzville like other small towns was too weak to stand the shock. Her industries were paralyzed and her businessmen scattered and at the end of the four years struggle her once happy and prosperous people returned to find the houses and business enterprises almost a wreck, and trade scattered to neighboring towns.

This would lead one to believe that during the Civil War, the town was almost abandoned, which may account for the report that when troops reached Wentzville in July 1861, the town was almost deserted.

Another story that might shed light on how zealous Krekel's Dutch German and other Union forces were in the area involves Emma S. English. Her family had moved to the Flint Hill area from New York when Emma was about six. So although she was a northerner, most of her friends and neighbors were southerners, and her older brother Lewis had joined Lee's army. In fact, it is believed that he fought with the Forty-Third Virginia Cavalry, also known as Moseley's Guerrillas. Emma English was confronted with taking the oath of allegiance; the provost marshal papers state, "[She] is a rebel on principle and to take oath would be to lie; declines to answer many questions. English's statement refuting the charges against her; she is a southern sympathizer but no rebel although she will assist them; will not go south." In *U.S. vs English*, English was called "a bad and defiant rebel; received rebel mail; implicated in bushwhacker attempt in Wright City, Warren County." She was arrested as a result, and while not confined to jail, she was banished from Missouri and had to report to the authorities. The reports of the provost marshal show her reporting from Michigan and, finally, Vermont, where she spent the remainder of the war. In March 1864, she petitioned the government to be allowed to come home to Missouri. She was eventually allowed to return and later married a widower, Thompson Cox, and had two children.

Chapter 3

Tobacco in St. Charles County and Wentzville

Tobacco in St. Charles County and Wentzville

By Lois Kessler, September 2024

When you think of farming in the Wentzville area, I am sure you think of corn, wheat, soybeans and cattle. Tobacco is associated with the South, not Missouri. But back in the 1800s, tobacco in this area was the crop of choice. You could say tobacco was king.

Before the Louisiana Purchase, this area was owned by Spain. Spain offered Daniel Boone a tract of land if he would settle the area and bring one hundred families with him. The families Daniel Boone brought were from Virginia, North Carolina, Kentucky and Tennessee. They were tobacco growers, and many were slave owners. Every farmer grew tobacco in some quantity; it

Tobacco plants being checked by a team from the Agricultural Extension Office, October 13, 1945. *Missouri Ruralist Photographs (P0030-0482b); SHSMO-Columbia.*

Omar Niederjohn growing tobacco in the 1920s–30s. *WCHS Collection.*

was considered a profitable crop. Slave labor was thought to have made it so. It is interesting to note that in Wentzville, the tobacco business continued to flourish at least twenty years after the Civil War and emancipation. In fact, in the early 1870s, Missouri ranked third in the production of tobacco in the United States. Western St. Charles County was considered one of the more productive regions. But production did fall from a high of 86,350 pounds in 1860 to 28,418 in 1880, one-third of what had been grown in 1860. The blame for this decline does not rest solely on emancipation. There was the great plug war, which was a result of James Duke embarking on eliminating the competition by cutting prices and extensive advertising. Pests and disease also contributed to the decline. Furthermore, tobacco depletes the soil of nutrients. Farmers at the time were not rotating crops, so much of the land could no longer support the growth of tobacco.

Wentzville is in Cuivre Township. The other two townships in Western St. Charles County are Callaway and Femme Osage. In 1860, the three top tobacco producers in Cuivre Township were William Scott, Eliza Carter and H.F. Elliot. Of these three, only Eliza was a slaveholder. However, it is possible that the other two rented slave labor. So the drop in production from 1860 to 1880 is probably due in part to the loss of enslaved labor. In 1880, the top producers in Cuivre Township were Alexander Boyd, Charles Allen, William Baker, John O'Brien, Joseph Farris and George Jenkins. In total, these farmers produced 14,200 pounds of tobacco, half of all the tobacco grown in the township.

To support the growing industry, tobacco barns and tobacco factories were built, and tobacco companies were organized. While the tobacco industry in Wentzville was short-lived (from approximately 1850 through 1880, only thirty years), many of the people we associate with the early tobacco companies got their start and training in the Wentzville area.

During this time, at least eleven different factories operated in Wentzville. Foristell, known as Millville at the time, is known to have had three factories. Flint Hill is known to have had at least one factory, and Wright City had a large factory. The amount of tobacco these factories processed was more than what was produced in Western St. Charles County, so the factories must have been buying tobacco from all over the state or country, maybe from overseas.

One of the products produced in Wentzville tobacco factories was plug tobacco. Plug tobacco is said to have originated with early settlers in Kentucky or Missouri. Cut tobacco was sweetened with honey and pressed into holes drilled in green maple or hickory logs. Wooden plugs were driven into the holes to compress the tobacco. The drying wood absorbed the excess moisture from the tobacco. Many articles I have read about the history of tobacco in St. Charles County credit the invention of plug chewing tobacco to Wentzville factories, or at least to St. Charles County factories. However, in my research, I have also found ads in St. Louis papers offering for auction kegs of Kentucky Plug Tobacco as early as 1816. So I find suspect the claim that Wentzville Factories invented plug tobacco; I can well imagine that our factories refined the process.

The image to the right shows three different stencils used on the packages of three different tobacco products made by the Wentzville Tobacco Co.

By the 1880s, plug tobacco was all the rage. As with any popular item, the counterfeiters got to work. The counterfeit plug tobacco was manufactured from brown paper and tobacco stems scented with licorice and painted with lamp black.

It was common to see women and children working in St. Louis tobacco factories. However, when looking at the census for Wentzville during these years, you'll see most women gave their occupation as homemaker; most men gave as their occupation farmer, tobacco factory worker or tobacconist. I did find evidence of children working in the factories. In 1870, one family had three daughters who each listed their occupation as tobacco factory worker. They ranged in age from eleven to fourteen. Also, in the 1870 census, William Muzzy, age eleven, listed his occupation as tobacco factory worker. His father and grandfather owned a factory.

The Wentzville Tobacco Company used these stencils to identify types of tobacco for sale. The original stencils were copper and eight by eighteen inches. *WCHS Collection.*

I must confess that before researching this article, I don't think I associated working in a tobacco factory with danger. But most tobacco factories employed hydraulic presses and pumps, cutters, flattening presses, iron finishers and steaming kettles and smoked the tobacco to enhance flavor. The process of producing plug tobacco included sorting the tobacco, stripping the stems and casing and rolling it in preparation for pressing it into cakes. It was a hot, dirty business. It also does not appear to have been a cheap business to enter. Yet in Wentzville, tobacco partnerships and factories seemed to pop up on a whim. Some of the factories and partnerships follow.

George S. Myers (later of Liggett and Myers fame) is thought to have had the first factory in Wentzville. This factory was in the vicinity of the home that, as of 2024, sits on the northwest corner of South Elm and Fourth Street. Myers also partnered with Benjamin Pearce (originally Pierce) and operated a factory near the "old Lutheran Parsonage." We believe this refers to the original Lutheran church in Wentzville, which was located on Pitman Avenue (originally Second Street, with the parsonage to the east). This partnership started in 1860 and produced fine-cut chewing and smoking tobacco. The factory burned down probably in 1861 or 1862, and Myers and Pearce moved to Alton, Illinois in 1862. The Civil War fighting in the area may have forced this move. They dissolved their partnership in 1863.

W.H. Savage and P.M. May had a factory on Mill Street (now Wall Street). Their factory building was later used as a flour mill, Peerless Flour Mill, and was later remodeled, becoming the home of the Clem Bauer family. May also operated a factory with his son-in-law W.H. Muzzy near the old Clobes residence (we are still researching where this home stood, but it may have been on West Main Street, possibly on the southwest corner of Church Street and West Main).

At different times, the Thompson Building, which stood on West Main Street where the Trinity Building (also known as the Southside Hotel) stands as of 2024 had a tobacco factory there. John Thompson and his brother Swan had built the hotel, and John operated a tobacco factory in the building. Later, John F. Bornhop, who is best known for being a postmaster and, later, the owner of the *Wentzville Union* in the 1920s and '30s, operated a cigar factory in the building. The building was never used as a hotel but was used as retail and office space and later burned down or was torn down. The building that stands there now was built at that location but on a smaller footprint.

Robert Dula and his father-in-law, Joel Carr, operated a factory in the building that was known as the Garment Factory. They also operated a

Top: This building was once a tobacco factory owned by W.H. Savage and P.M. May. It would later become Peerless Flour Mill. *WCHS Collection.*

Bottom: Clem Bauer's property on Wall Street was formerly Peerless Flour Mill in the 1870s–90s and was converted into a house. *WCHS Collection.*

This building was built in 1885 and was used as a tobacco factory, a milling company and, lastly, a garment factory. This image is dated 1970. *WCHS Collection.*

factory on the lot east of 408 East Main Street. Most of the Dula brothers were involved in the tobacco business in some fashion.

Paul Brown started in the tobacco business in 1865. In 1874, he formed a partnership with Wesley Sherman, F.H. Lacy, Lewis W. English and A.C. Hudson. They called the firm Sherman, Lacy & Brown. This group was very interrelated by marriage. Paul Brown's first wife was Martha Hudson; her brother was A.C. Hudson. Lewis English was married to Paul Brown's sister, and when she passed away, he married Laura Dula, one of the Dulas' sisters. In 1881, the firm became the Brown Co., Inc.

John and James T. Drummond formed the Drummond Tobacco Co. and operated a factory here. Father and son Hutton (Hut) and James Lacy had a factory west of 111 West Allen. Another father-son duo was Charles and John E. Richards. John was known as an expert tobacco roller. Dr. J.C. Goodrich and Joel Carr had a partnership in 1862. In 1859, S.A. Grantham was in the tobacco industry in the area.

While William M. Allen was not known to be in business operating any tobacco factories, I have seen documents and letters written by Allen to the Missouri Tobacco Board supporting different people at various times to be the local tobacco inspector. As stated earlier, during this time, it seems that everyone in the area was dealing in the tobacco business in some fashion.

Brief biographies of some of the people associated with the tobacco industry in the area follow. Joseph Goodrich, DDS, was also involved with tobacco; please read about him in chapter 4.

Dula Family Members of Wentzville Who Were Involved in Tobacco (Robert, Adolphus, Laura, Sidney and Caleb)

By Lois Kessler, October 2024

The Dula family first arrived in Wentzville when Sidney P . and Jane Connely Dula moved their family from Calwell County, North Carolina, in October 1870. Sidney and Jane had ten children, five boys and five girls. When they came to Missouri, their oldest child was twenty-three and the youngest was six. Their children, in order of birth, were:

1. George Thomas, born April 10, 1847, Lenoir, North Carolina; died March 15, 1912, Salisbury, North Carolina
2. Robert "Bob" Byron, born November 3, 1848, Lenoir, North Carolina; died April 27, 1926, New York, New York
3. Adolphus "Dolph" Washington, born December 30, 1849, Lenoir, North Carolina; died April 12, 1912, St. Louis, Missouri
4. Louise Adelaide "Addie," born July 2, 1852, Lenoir, North Carolina; died July 1887
5. Mary Elizabeth, also known as Myra, born June 1854, Lenoir, North Carolina; died 1925, Lenoir, North Carolina
6. Laura Jane, born November 28, 1856, Lenoir, North Carolina; died November 14, 1950, St. Louis, Missouri
7. Mattie, born 1858, North Carolina; died 1859, North Carolina
8. Ella M., born 1859, Lenoir, North Carolina; died 1891, Montgomery, Alabama
9. Sidney or Sydney Rutherford, born August 30, 1861, North Carolina; died July 10, 1930, Danville, Virginia
10. Caleb Conley, born 1864, Lenoir, North Carolina; died December 25, 1930, New York, New York

In Caldwell County, North Carolina, Dulas were plentiful. On both the mother's and father's side, their ancestors were colonial families in the area.

They were descendants of Reverend Dr. John Witherspoon, president of Princeton College and a signer of the Declaration of Independence for the State of New Jersey. They boast several ancestors who fought in the American Revolution.

It was after the revolution that Dula ancestors moved from Virginia to North Carolina and Georgia. For the most part, the Dulas were farmers, plantation owners, with vast landholdings. One branch of the family in Lenoir, North Carolina, is credited with developing an apple called the Dula Beauty.

In some areas of North Carolina, an *a* at the end of a word is pronounced *ee*, so in those areas, *Dula* may have been pronounced *Dulee*. In fact, the Georgia Dulas started spelling their name Dooley. Don't think that all their ancestors and relatives were upstanding citizens. Remember the song "Hang Down Your Head Tom Dooley" by the Kingston Trio? The song is about Tom Dula from Lenoir, North Carolina, who was accused of murdering a girl and hanged for the offence. Tom was a cousin of the Dulas.

Sidney was a wealthy planter. In 1849, running as a Whig, Sidney was elected clerk of courts in Caldwell County Court, North Carolina. Later, he would be affiliated with the Democratic Party. He held the clerk of courts position until the Civil War. Sidney also believed in education and was a trustee of Valley Academy in Caldwell County and on the board of Davenport Female College in Lenoir, North Carolina. He was a man who believed in temperance.

Sidney, like most of the Dulas, was a slaveholder, and in 1861, he helped form troops that became Company I of the Twenty-Sixth Regular North Carolina troops that fought under General Robert E. Lee. He was a first lieutenant and one of the first men to volunteer.

At the start of the Civil War, the Dula sons were too young to serve in the military. But George and Robert volunteered for the North Carolina Home Guard in Caldwell County, North Carolina. The duties of the home guard were to guard against invaders and to round up Confederate deserters and draftees. They were known as the boy soldiers. The boys were seventeen and fifteen.

The end of the Civil War found the Dulas' lives much altered. Their plantation was in ruins, their Confederate money was worthless and they couldn't pay their taxes. Some reports indicate that in October 1867, Robert set out on horseback, going west, and after a month he arrived in Flint Hill. This would suggest he was sent as a scout for his family. His parents settled their affairs in North Carolina and, in October 1870, left with their family for Missouri. It is unclear why they came to Missouri and to the Wentzville area, but it is possible that they already had a cousin or other relatives or friends in the area. Some accounts say that the oldest son, George, remained in Anson County, but there is evidence that while he did return there, he did for a short time stay in Missouri. Sidney and Jane were able to buy or rent some land, and Sidney started growing tobacco. The farm was described as on a "post oak ridge" between Wentzville and Flint Hill.

In January 1876, Sidney P. was on his way to Sunday school in Wentzville, where he was the Sunday school superintendent, when he fell from his horse and broke his leg badly. He died of complications from the broken leg on February 11, 1876. Not long after Sidney's passing, Jane passed away, on May 27, 1876. Her obituary mentions her husband's death and refers to them both as "aged and respected." Jane was forty-nine, and Sidney was just shy of turning fifty-one. All their life, Sidney and Jane were community-minded and active both in their communities and their church. Their children did the same.

After the death of Sidney P. Dula, a paper in North Carolina announced his death and had this to say: "Sidney Dula died at his home near Wentzville, MO, whither he had moved about 6 years ago to try to retrieve his lost fortune and find a home for his children which move has resulted in disappointment and irretrievable loss to all." Of course, the writer did not have a crystal ball, so he didn't know what fate had in store for Sidney's children. The writer went on to say: "I do not say he was perfect, but I do say I never knew a more perfect model of Christian Gentleman in all his deportment….[He was] never known to utter a profane word."

At the time of Sidney and Jane's deaths, all their children were married except the three youngest: Ella, Sidney and Caleb. Ella went to live with her sister Myra and her family in Cameron, Missouri. The two boys lived with Robert and his family in Wentzville.

According to the 1880 census, most men and children in Wentzville were involved the tobacco industry as tobacconists, salesmen, cigar makers and tobacco factory workers. The Dula brothers were no exception; they, too, were in the tobacco business. While all the sons became involved with the tobacco industry, only one daughter married into the tobacco industry. This chapter concentrates on the tobacco/Wentzville connection, so only the Dula children involved with tobacco are discussed.

Robert "Bob" Byron, Second Son/Child

Robert Byron, the second-born son (also known as R.D. and called Bob by his friends), on arrival in the Wentzville area, worked on a farm, taught school for a couple of years near Flint Hill and during, the summer, sold tobacco for Joel Carr. Bob also clerked in a local store owned by Paul Brown and for seven years worked as a traveling salesmen selling tobacco. In 1874, Bob married Joel Carr's daughter Josephine, who was born and raised in Wentzville (1856–1929). Their first four children, three girls and a boy, were born while they lived in Wentzville. Another daughter and son would join the family after they left Wentzville.

Portrait of Robert Dula, 1904. *Courtesy of St. Louis Public Library Digital Collection, Identifier D82900.*

After the marriage, Dula and Carr formed a partnership and operated a tobacco factory in Wentzville. Bob and Josephine were active in the Wentzville Dramatic Society. Bob served as a manager of the society. The society preformed plays not only in Wentzville but also in St. Charles and St. Louis. Bob and Josephine were also active, along with their oldest daughters, in the Wentzville Musical Literary Club. Bob was known as a fine vocalist.

In 1881, while still in Wentzville, Bob Dula was granted his first patent. It was for a funnel for filling sacks or bags and packing smoking tobacco. In 1882, he and Joel Carr got a trademark for plug and other chewing tobacco. Dula has at least seven patents in his name; most are for machines or processes used in the tobacco industry. One was for a coin-operated machine that would dispense "cigarette packages" or other items. That's right: a vending machine. His last patent was not for anything related to tobacco; it was for concrete blocks.

All his life, Bob, like his parents, was very community-minded, active in his church and in public affairs. Two examples of his involvement are from when he lived in Wentzville. During the Wentzville fire of 1882, while fighting the fire, Bob acted as the fire chief, directing people on what to do. After the big Wentzville fire in 1882, he was also on the committee to get donations to rebuild.

In May 1883, before FEMA and public assistance, a large tornado went through Wentzville. The track of the storm was almost half a mile wide for thirty miles. Newspaper reports at the time said, "Many families have not a change of clothing, no food, no shelter, no houses. They are almost as naked and destitute as when they came into the world." Mayor J.C. Goodrich appointed a three-man committee (Robert B. Dula, J.C. Johnson and Charles Walker) to seek aid. They, in turn, appointed Garner Hitch to solicit donations from St. Louis.

In 1884, Bob, along with A.A. Meyer and A. Stonebraker, filed articles of association with the State of Missouri for the St. Charles Tobacco Company, with $50,000 in capital and stock half paid up. Also, in April that year, Bob and Joel Carr sold lot 4, block 7 in Wentzville to the St. Charles Tobacco Company for $8,500.

In 1884, James T. Drummond, who had noticed how well Carr and Dula Tobacco Company was operated, asked Bob to become the general manager for Drummond Tobacco Company. At the time, Drummond Tobacco employed four thousand people and processed sixty million pounds of tobacco a year. It was considered the largest manufacturer of its kind in the world.

The family moved to St. Louis. While in St. Louis, Bob was involved not only in tobacco but also in real estate (as a buyer, seller and developer), banking, disaster relief, mining and politics. He served on the school board

Robert Dula's St. Louis home at 4171 Bell Street. *Courtesy of Missouri Historical Society, Identifier N06259.*

and on grand juries, as a director of other companies and as a director of the committee that planned the 1904 world's fair.

During his time in St. Louis, Bob dealt with worker strikes, and because of his stance on unions, he was considered their enemy. His job had him constantly traveling to New York, North Carolina, Kentucky, Ohio, Virginia and other states. In 1890, to travel, you went by train, boat, or horse. During this time, a train trip from St. Louis to New York took at least twenty-two hours. You wonder how there were enough hours in the day to do everything, yet Bob still found time for his favorite leisure pursuits, golf and fishing.

In 1895, along with H.I. Drummond and Clarence Jones, Bob formed the Western Cigarette Machine Company. Drummond and Bob secured the rights to the Elliot cigarette machine, which was the only cigarette-rolling machine not controlled by what was known as the tobacco trust (the largest tobacco companies). In addition to the other tobacco products they were already manufacturing, they also got into the machine-made cigarette business.

By 1896, Bob was the second vice president of Drummond Tobacco Company, and in 1898, he became first vice president. In 1899, the company was sold to American Tobacco Company, which was part of the tobacco trust. The tobacco trust also acquired Liggett and Myers Tobacco Company the same year, and Dula was appointed managing director of Liggett & Myers Drummond Branch. According to the *National Cyclopedia of American Biography*, Bob continued to rise in the ranks because his "superior executive abilities became manifest, and his comprehensive grasp of the business made his office one of the most important in the organization."

The amount of money tobacco companies generated and the amount of tobacco they processed daily is astounding. During this time, tobacco factories were the major employer in St. Louis. Of course, some of that money flowed to the Dulas, along with the money his other enterprises were generating. The Dulas' houses became fancier; their kids went to private schools on the East Coast. They spent summers at fancy resorts. They attended balls and charity events, had box seats at various functions and the horse races. The St. Louis society pages were full of their social activities. In 1896, Bob was a founding member of an organization called Veterans of the Blue and Grey. The organization was for veterans who fought on either side during the Civil War. Its purpose was to show that the war was over, both sides could—and did—work together and the United States should never be divided again. During this time, Josephine was very active in the Daughters of the Confederacy and the DAR and on the board of the Blind

Girls School. Yet even with all this, the Dulas were considered to have simple taste, and Bob was described as having a "quiet demeanor."

In December 1900, Bob formed the Conejo Mining Company with $400,000 in paid capital. The other investors were Paul Brown, Walter Brown, Lewis English (his brother-in-law) and Maurice Clark.

By 1901, Bob was the local director of the tobacco trust. He and Josephine became original members of the Glen Echo Country Club. Glen Echo Country Club is the oldest golf club west of the Mississippi River and has been in continuous operation at the same location since its founding. In 1904, Glen Echo hosted the 1904 Olympic Golf Games.

By 1903, Bob was VP of operations. According to his obituary published in *Tobacco*, an industry trade paper, he held this position because of "his knowledge of the leaf and of manufacturing methods, and his ability to develop young men." The obituary goes on to say, "He became closely associated with American Tobacco President James B. Duke and played an important part in the company's growth." In 1904, it was announced that he and his family were moving to New York and would be selling their house and its furnishings in St. Louis. While in New York, they lived on Park Avenue and had a country estate they called Hibriten, after Hibriten Mountain, which overlooked Bob's hometown, Lenoir, North Carolina. The estate was over 170 acres; included Greystone Castle, built by Standard Oil associate Josiah Macy Jr.; and is part of Lyndhurst Estate owned by Helen Gould. Once again, the family was very involved in the local social scene.

On July 2, 1890, the federal government passed the Sherman Anti-Trust Act. When Teddy Roosevelt ran for president, his campaign was called the Trust Busting Campaign. Roosevelt saw things as good or bad: i.e., good trust or bad trust. In 1902, he started using executive orders to go up against trusts he saw as bad. During this time, the courts and the public looked favorably on busting up trusts. The first to fall, in 1904, was Northern Securities (a railroad trust). Next, the government went after Standard Oil and the American Tobacco Company trust. The suit against the tobacco trust started in 1907. During that time, some speculated that Bob, his brother Caleb and Paul Brown might be sent to prison along with other tobacco men.

The Supreme Court's 1911 ruling in *United States v. American Tobacco Co.* stated that the combination of the tobacco companies "in and of itself, as well as each and all of the elements composing it whether corporate or individual, whether considered collectively or separately [was] in restraint

Left: Robert Dula's New York house. *Google Earth.*

Below: Robert Dula is in the back row, second from right. His wife, Josephine (Carr), is the lady in the black hat behind the woman who's turning around. Robert Dula Jr. is in the back row, first on the left. Caleb Dula, Robert's brother, is in the first row of men, second from left. *WCHS Collection.*

of trade and an attempt to monopolize, and a monopolization within the first and second sections of the Anti-Trust Act." But it was not a unanimous decision. The result was to break the trust into four companies: American Tobacco Company, R.J. Reynolds, Liggett & Myers and Lorillard. This was accomplished mainly by the redistribution and reissuing of stock. While the monopoly became an oligopoly, much of its management did not change. Bob became a director of Liggett & Myers, while his brother Caleb became president of the same company. In 1911, Bob retired from being active in the tobacco industry and concentrated on his real estate holdings.

Caleb Dula is in the center of this picture, taken at his New York house. Caleb was the first president of Liggett and Myers Tobacco Company. *WCHS Collection.*

Bob and Josephine made frequent trips to Wentzville over the years to visit her mother, Fannie Carr, who lived on Wall Street along with her sisters and brothers, and Bob's brother Adolphus.

Bob died on April 27, 1926, at his home on Park Avenue in New York City. He was remembered as a "most companionable gentleman, not at all spoiled by his success, but unassuming and genial to a rare degree. He [was] a good storyteller and [had] the rare facility of enjoying the other fellow's joke." His will left all his money to his five living children. It went on to state that his wife had been provided for previously. His estate was valued between $1.3 and $2 million. Today, the estate would be worth between $23 and $35 million. At the time of his death, Bob and Josephine were being sued by their youngest son Robert L.'s wife, who accused them of alienation of affection. For this reason, Robert's L.'s share was left in a trust. After Bob's death, their ex-daughter-in-law was awarded $100,000 by the courts.

Josephine passed away on November 15, 1929, in New York. Her estate was estimated between $2 and $3 million, which in today's dollars would be about $53 million. She left the bulk of her estate to her children, but Robert L.'s inheritance was reduced by $65,000, an amount she said was due his father. She did leave money or trusts to her brothers and sisters and a couple of her granddaughters. Bob and Josephine are buried in the family mausoleum in Woodlawn Cemetery in the Bronx.

Adolphus "Dolph" Dula, Third Son/Child

Adolphus Washington Dula was born on December 30, 1849. Adolphus was the third son of Sidney and Jane Dula. He was called Dolph by family and friends. I have seen articles suggesting that Adolphus and Bob were twins, but in fact, Bob was thirteen months older than Adolphus. On July 26, 1876, two months after the death of his mother, Dolph married Georgianna Adams. Georgianna's family was from the Carolinas, but at the time of their marriage, her family was living five miles north of Foristell. When the 1883 tornado previously mentioned went through the Foristell area, Georgianna's parents' home was one of those that were severely damaged.

The 1880 census shows Adolphus and his family living in the Wentzville area; Adolphus was a farmer. It's possible that, as the oldest son living at home when his parents died, Adolphus took over his parents' farm.

By 1886, if not before, Adolphus had given up farming and was working as a "commercial traveler" a.k.a. "drummer" a.k.a. salesman for Drummond Tobacco Company, selling cigars and other tobacco products. He was considered a popular salesman, and his territory covered Louisiana, Ohio, Missouri, Arkansas and Kansas. Adolphus was on the road constantly. His one outlet was being a member of the Wentzville Masonic Lodge. Meanwhile, Georgianna stayed home and raised their six children: three boys and three girls. Often, Dula nieces and nephews would visit their home in Wentzville.

In 1905, Adolphus and Georgianna decided to sell their home in Wentzville and move to St. Louis. They sold their home on South East Main (now 408 East Main) to John Brown and his wife. It included the lot on either side of the home. Brown at one time was the mayor of Wentzville. Adolphus and Georgianna moved to Folsom Avenue in St. Louis. They might have made this move because all three of their oldest sons were no longer living at home. Their daughter Emma was married, living in St. Louis and had just had her second child; their daughter Josephine was married and living in Mexico, Missouri; and their daughter Mamie had married the principal of the

Wentzville school and recently moved to Oklahoma Indian Territory. Plus, their son Ralph had gotten a job in charge of one of the leaf departments at American Tobacco Co. in St. Louis.

On Saturday, December 22, 1906, Ralph went shopping with his mother. On Sunday, December 23, he went on a walk on Grand Avenue and bought a newspaper. At three o'clock that afternoon, he lay down for a brief nap and told his mother that his legs felt paralyzed and he thought he needed a doctor. A little later, he told his mother things were going black and he needed a doctor immediately He died shortly thereafter. It was thought he had suffered a heart attack. He was twenty years old. Ralph was laid to rest in Linn Cemetery with his Adams grandparents.

Adolphus died on April 12, 1912. He was laid to rest in Linn Cemetery in Wentzville with his son.

Sadly, about 1916, Adolphus and Georgianna's oldest son, Sidney, who was married and had three children, was diagnosed with dementia praecox psychosis, today known as schizophrenia. He was committed to the state hospital in Farmington and would live there for forty years.

Georgianna was living with a daughter in Springfield, Missouri, when she passed away on March 4, 1923. After a funeral in Springfield, her body was shipped to Wentzville and buried next to her husband and son in Linn Cemetery.

Laura Dula, Third Daughter and Sixth Child

Laura Dula married Lewis W. English in Wentzville in 1882. Lewis's first wife was Lucy Brown; her brother was Paul Brown, one of the well-known tobacco factory owners in Wentzville. Lucy died in 1877 while giving birth to the couple's fourth daughter. The daughter also died. Lucy and her daughter were buried in the Methodist Cemetery in Flint Hill.

Lewis English was born in New York in 1842, the second son of Charles and Clarissa Crittenden English. Sometime between 1845 and 1851, Charles moved his family to Flint Hill, Missouri, where his brother Benjah was a doctor. Soon after arriving in Missouri, Charles Sr. and his oldest son, Charles Jr., left for the goldfields of California to make their fortune. This left his mother, Clarissa, to fend for herself with two young sons and four daughters; the oldest was only sixteen. In 1855, while still in California, Charles Jr. drowned.

In 1856, Clarissa English passed away. She is buried in the Methodist Cemetery in Flint Hill. Her youngest son was five years old when she died. The 1860 census found the family scattered. Lewis was living in St. Charles and working at the courthouse. Sister Emma was living with Paul and Lucy Brown's mother and stepfather; she listed her occupation as cigar maker. Sister Cora was living with her half-sister Elizabeth and her family. It is unknown where the remainder of the family was living in 1860.

When the Civil War started, Lewis joined the Confederate army. It is believed that he might have been part of the Forty-Third Virginia Cavalry, also known as Moseley's Guerrillas. It was during this time that his sister Emma was arrested for alleged treason, and while not imprisoned, she was exiled from Missouri and obliged to report to the authorities on a regular basis. She was moved to Michigan and then, finally, to Vermont where she spent the remainder of the war.

After the war, Lewis's father, Charles, returned to Missouri from California in bad health, but he never lived with his family again. At the same time, after the war, Lewis tried his hand at being a river boat captain, and in 1867, he married Lucy Brown, Paul Brown's younger sister.

Around 1874, Lewis went to work for his brother-in-law Paul Brown and Jim Lacey in their tobacco factory in Wentzville as a bookkeeper. When the Paul Brown factory moved to Montgomery City, Lewis went with them, in the capacity of treasurer. His half-sister Elizabeth went with him to take care of his daughters. The town of Montgomery City offered Brown and Lacy, the owners of the tobacco factory, a hefty cash bonus to move the business there. Lewis remained a widow for five years, raising his three daughters with the help of his sister in Montgomery City.

In 1882, Lewis married Laura Dula; they lived in Montgomery City. Right after his marriage to Laura, Lewis left on an extended trip out west in the interest of the firm. In 1885, in Montgomery City, Lewis and Laura had a son; they named him Fred.

In 1894, Lacy & Brown Tobacco Factory moved their operation to St. Louis. The English family also moved to St. Louis, except for Lewis's daughter Cora, who married in 1890 and remained in Montgomery City. In fact, since all the daughters had been raised mainly in Montgomery City, all would eventually marry in that area and stay.

In 1900, while living in St. Louis and working still for the tobacco company, Lewis was involved in the incorporation of two mining companies. In January 1900, Lewis, C.E. Flack, W.W. Gregg and others incorporated the Portland Mining Co. of St. Louis. This company started mining in the

Kansas City area. In December the same year, Lewis, along with Robert Dula, Paul Brown, Walter Brown and Maurice Clark, incorporated the Conejo Mining Company with $400,000 in capital.

In June 1901, the *Wentzville Union* reported that Lewis and Laura visited Wentzville and Montgomery City before he left for "old Mexico," where he was interested in gold mining. He went to Oaxaca, Mexico, where he was the resident manager of a mining operation for Conejo Mining. While mining had gone on in that region for centuries, for the first time, speculators were bringing in big equipment to mine. It is unclear if Laura was with him during this time or if she stayed in the States. By August 1902, Lewis was back in Missouri.

By 1905, Laura resigned from several committees, the reason being "they have to go south for her husband's health." In May 1906, while Lewis is traveling by train from Los Angeles to the Redlands to meet a friend, he suffered a stroke and was taken to the Good Samaritan Hospital in Los Angeles. After suffering a series of strokes, Lewis died on August 22, 1906. Laura had his body taken back to Wentzville, and after a funeral at the Methodist church, Lucy buried him in Flint Hill.

In 1943, their son Fred, who was a lawyer, dies of bacterial endocarditis. He was buried in St. Louis. Laura never remarried. When she died on November 14, 1950, she had been a widow for forty-four years. She was ninety-four and outlived her husband, all her brothers and sisters, her son and a stepdaughter. Laura is buried in the Methodist Cemetery in Flint Hill with Lewis and his family.

Sidney R., Fourth Son and Ninth Child

Sydney Rutherford (whose friends called him Ralph but who usually went by his middle name, Rutherford), was superintendent of the St. Charles Tobacco Company in 1886 and living in St. Charles, Missouri. In 1888, he was in Danville, Virginia, for a short period of time as a buyer. In 1889, he was living in Henderson, Kentucky, and was the superintendent of Hodge Tobacco Co. In November 1889, he married Gaberiella Madison Hart in Louisville, Kentucky. Gaberiella's friends and family called her Ella. Unlike most of the Dula sisters and wives, who didn't work outside the home, Ella continued to work as a bookkeeper at least until 1900.

Around 1890, Danville, Virginia was seen by Sidney R. and his brother Caleb as the predominate tobacco market in the area, so they went to Danville with their wives and established a branch of the Drummond Tobacco Company. Danville would become the largest and best loose leaf tobacco market in the States. Danville historians claim that from 1890 until their deaths, Sidney R. and Ella made their home in Danville, but I have found evidence that between the years 1890 and 1896, Sidney R. and Ella, at various times, made their home in Henderson, Kentucky; St. Louis, Missouri; Montgomery City, Missouri; and Winston, Kentucky. But it may be these were temporary assignments and they always called Danville home. Sidney R. was known as a leaf dealer and a buyer of fine wrappers.

Shortly after the brothers arrived in Danville, Caleb began construction of two identical houses that sat side by side at 1027 and 1031 Main Street. Sidney R. and Ella would live at 1027 until 1909, when they sold the home and moved to 936 Main Street. It is believed that Caleb and wife, Julia, lived in 1031 until Caleb was called back to St. Louis by the company.

Like his brothers, Sidney R. was active in religious, civic and city affairs, and while he was a Democrat, he was not very involved in politics. Like his two very successful brothers Robert and Caleb, he was involved in other businesses: he served on the board of a bank and president of a pants factory and owned several business buildings in Danville. Likewise, Ella was active in religious, social and intellectual organizations: she served on the boards of various benevolent societies and was considered the founder of the Danville Garden Club.

While Sidney R. was not as rich or successful as his brothers Bob and Caleb, he and Ella lived a comfortable life. They spent summers at Virginia Beach, had a chauffeur and servants and were very active in Danville social life. Caleb visited often, as did other family members from both sides.

In October 1928, Ella passed away. Sidney R. died in July 1930. They are buried in the family mausoleum they share with one of Ella's sisters and her husband. At the time of Sidney R.'s death, only two of his siblings were still alive: his sister Laura and his brother Caleb. Sidney R. died intestate, leaving an estate valued at $242,000. Laura was the administrator, but since she lived in St. Louis, she had to post a $225,000 bond. His estate was divided between Laura, Caleb and all his living nieces and nephews.

CALEB DULA, YOUNGEST SON AND TENTH CHILD

Caleb was the youngest son of Sidney and Jane Dula and their tenth child. He was born in 1864. After his parents' death in 1876, he and his brother Sidney R. moved in with their older brother Robert and his family. Sidney R. and Caleb would remain close all their lives, and Caleb and Julia visited Sidney R. and his wife, Ella, often in Danville, Virginia. At the age of twelve, Caleb started his career in tobacco; his first job was sorting tobacco leaves. According to the 1880 census, at sixteen, he was working in a tobacco factory in Wentzville.

In 1885, while living in St. Charles and working in the tobacco industry, Caleb married a Wentzville girl, Julia Womack. Julia's stepfather was the dentist Dr. Goodrich. In 1886, at the age of twenty-two, Caleb was working as a tobacco buyer. In 1886, he became an officer of the Drummond Tobacco Co. In 1890, along with his brother Sidney R., he and Julia moved to Danville, Virginia, and they established the firm of Carr and Dula. In 1909, an assassination plot to kill various members of the Chicago Stock Exchange was uncovered. Caleb was one of the members on the list.

Caleb's rise in the tobacco industry was rapid. In 1899, he moved to New York as a department manager for the American Tobacco Co, and by 1911, after the antitrust suit, he'd been named president of Liggett & Myers. He was forty-seven. An article published in the *St. Louis Star and Times* called him a "natural born hustler." Caleb also held strong views on what led to success and what led to poverty. He believed that the man who stayed in one industry and with one company got ahead, unlike the man who went from job to job solely for the reason of a slightly larger paycheck.

Caleb and Julia had no children, but Julia's niece and her family lived with them for many years. Caleb was like his brother Robert in many ways. He was civic-minded: for example, during World War I, he bought over $60,000 in liberty bonds and donated $15,000 to the Red Cross. Later, he donated over $200,000 to Duke University for its endowment fund, along with several famous paintings. He donated his time and money toward establishing a YMCA in both Yonkers and Danville, Virginia. He was on the boards of several large and small businesses and gave to many charities and relief funds. He also, at various times, gave donations to both Republican and Democratic candidates. Before her death, Julia established the Caleb and Julia W. Dula Educational Charitable Foundation, leaving an endowment of over $3.8 million. The fund was to be used for religious, educational, charitable and scientific purposes.

Caleb was interested in horticulture and played an active part in establishing the Boyce-Thompson Plant Institute. He was an avid hunter and golfer and founded the Hudson River Country Club. Like his brother Robert, he owned a country estate. His estate overlooked the Hudson River and was known as Lenoir. Also like his brother Robert, he was an inventor, holding ten patents to his name, all related to the tobacco business.

Caleb died on December 25, 1930, at his home in New York. He was the last of the Dula brothers who had called Wentzville home. On his death, his only sibling still living was Laura Dula English. His estate, which was worth almost $2 million, was left to his wife, Julia. Nine years later, Julia died, on August 11, 1939; by then, the estate was valued at over $15 million. Julia left her estate to family and a lifelong friend who had been her bridesmaid at her wedding all those many years ago. Caleb and Julia are buried in the family mausoleum in Sleepy Hollow Cemetery in Sleepy Hollow, New York.

John F. Bornhop: Tobacco Man, Postmaster, Justice of the Peace and Editor

By Gerry Matlock

Originally published in the Wentzville Union*, August 25, 1976*

The estate of John F. Bornhop of Wentzville was auctioned last week, and hundreds of people purchased relics of the past accumulated since the 1880s. So much mystery was present as I searched through the numerous items to be auctioned. It prompted me to research our history and tell the story of this gentleman so that we may pay tribute to him and pass on the story of his life. Although his relics are gone forever and distributed across the country, his deeds will be remembered through this story.

John was born at Schoenberg, in the province of Schleswig-Holstein, Germany, on March 22, 1856, and died at Wentzville on June 23, 1933 (a full seventy-seven years). His parents were Christian and Bertha Dierks Von Bahrenhoff, anglicized as Bornhop.

John came to America at the age of eighteen and lived with his uncle John Bornhop on a farm near Davenport, Iowa. His foot, injured at a Turnverein Hall in Germany, was reinjured while on the farm, necessitating amputation of his right foot. Handicapped, he faced life bravely and went to St. Louis,

where he resided until 1881. At this time, he relocated to Wentzville and was employed by the Savage and May Tobacco Company.

On June 23, 1886, he was married to Miss Wilhelmina Catherine Clobes, who was born in Wentzville on June 1, 1861. Wilhelmina's father, William Clobes, was born in Hesse-Kassel, Germany, and migrated to America in 1853, locating in New Melle. In 1857, Mr. Clobes moved to Warrenton and accepted employment with Charles Ober, where he learned the shoemaker trade and applied for citizenship papers. Mr. Ober was the grandfather of Vera Heidfmann Diekroeger. Mr. Clobes was married to Miss Margretha Gluck of St. Louis in 1860 and established his home in Wentzville. He started the first shoemaker shop here and operated it until his death in 1904.

His wife's mother, Margretha Gluck Clobes, was born in Hesse-Darmstadt, Germany. Five children were born to Mr. and Mrs. Clobes. Two died in infancy. The remaining children are Wilhelmina Catherine (Minnie; Mrs. J.F. Bornhop), William Clobes and Andrew Clobes. Mrs. Clobes died in February 1904, and Mr. Clobes followed her in July the same year.

John Bornhop became assistant postmaster from 1897 until 1914, when he became postmaster here in Wentzville. He was also justice of the peace of Cuivre Township for many years.

Opposite: John Bornhop, age unknown, and his wife, Minnie Clobes, eighteen. *WCHS Collection.*

Left: Mr. and Mrs. William Clobes, parents of Wilhelmina Bornhop, wife of John Bornhop. William Clobes moved to Wentzville in 1860 and started the first shoemaker's shop.

Below: John Bornhop, Wentzville's postmaster in the early 1900s, standing in front of the post office. *WCHS Collection.*

In October 1917, Mr. Bornhop purchased the *Wentzville Union*, which he published until his death in 1933. Mrs. J.F. Bornhop was her husband's companion and helpmate, having been assistant postmaster and news reporter until his death in 1933.

There were five children born to Mr. and Mrs. Bornhop: Gretha (Mrs. O.A. Wilson), Carrye (Mrs. C.S. Sidebottoms), Rosetta Bornhop, Andrew Bornhop and Oralee Bornhop. Mrs. Bornhop was a member of the Methodist Church, Eastern Star, Pollyanna Club and Royal Neighbors and always took an active interest in community life.

Left: The Bornhop family standing outside their home in Wentzville. *WCHS Collection.*

Right: John Bornhop attending to his beehives, a hobby he enjoyed. *WCHS Collection.*

John F. Bornhop united with the Evangelical Church when a small lad and, in 1906, joined the Wentzville M.E. Church South. Throughout his entire life, he was a lover of nature and of Nature's God, never so happy as when working with his flowers, garden and bees. John's passion was beekeeping. He kept hives and sold honey. The image at the right above shows a picture of John Bornhop with his favorite hobby. He was a member of the Masonic Lodge, of which he had been Worshipful Master of the Eastern Star and of which he had been Worthy Patron several times, and a member of the Modern Woodmen of America, and he formerly belonged to the Ancient Order of United Workmen (AOUW).

He belonged to that great company of superior German folk who have contributed so much to the building of St. Louis city, St. Louis County and St. Charles County. He bore his infirmity with patience and from boyhood, when he came to the United States, thrown upon his own resources, he made his way in this world. He had his struggles, hardships, sufferings and sorrows. He was never rich in this world's goods. He learned through diligent toil, frugality and economy life's real values. Because of his difficulty in getting about, he was not much on the public streets. His path for years was from his home gate to his place of business. Yet no man was truer to community welfare or thought more about civic improvement and the uplift of his fellowman.

Benjamin C. Pearce

By Kathy Weindel

Benjamin C. Pearce's story began in 1675, when his paternal great-great-grandfather, Gideon Pearce, emigrated from England and settled in the colony of Maryland on Chesapeake Bay. Gideon's grandson, Thomas Pearce Sr., and his third wife, Ann Evert, had five children, including Pearce's father, Thomas Pearce Jr. Pearce's father married Catharine Comegys in 1780. Pearce was born on October 10, 1813, the youngest of ten children born to Thomas and Catherine. In 1818, when Pearce was five, his family left Maryland and immigrated to what would become known as St. Charles County in Missouri.

Between 1832 and 1835, Pearce and his father purchased land between Wentzville and Flint Hill, Missouri, from the federal government. On their lands, Pearce and his father grew primarily tobacco, using enslaved laborers to cultivate the crops until the end of the Civil War.

Between 1831 and 1857 (according to his own account, while testifying as a witness in a murder trial in 1854), Pearce spent some "on and off" six years living in other parts of the country. It appears he spent four to five years of those years living in the Iowa Territory. In the first census taken in the territory, in 1836, Pearce was listed as a resident of the community of Dubuque. In 1839, he married Martha A.L. Camp, daughter of Hosea T. Camp, a member of the Iowa territorial government until his death in 1836 or 1837. In the 1840 U.S. census, Pearce was also listed as resident of Dubuque, and the census indicated that he employed at least two people as laborers, which leads to the assumption that he was farming during his time in Iowa.

In 1841, Pearce returned to St. Charles County, Missouri. He built his growing family a large brick home on his land two miles northeast of Wentzville on the road to Flint Hill. Between 1841 and 1858, Pearce and his wife raised six children. During these years, Pearce pursued the business of growing tobacco on his one-thousand-acre farm, using slave labor until after the Civil War. He and his neighbors made use of the North Missouri Railroad to ship their tobacco to St. Louis and other major cities, where it could be processed into tobacco products such as chewing tobacco or smokeless tobacco strips.

In addition to growing tobacco, Pearce pursued business partnerships with friends, neighbors and local businessmen. In 1859, he purchased land along what is presently known as Wall Street in Wentzville, Missouri, and built a factory.

In 1860 Pearce formed a partnership with Pinckney May, son of Charles May, and started a tobacco business in Wentzville. Their factory manufactured fine-cut chewing and smoking tobacco. Unfortunately, after the outbreak of the Civil War, guerilla and military clashes between Union troops and Southern sympathizers threatened their business. By 1863, Pearce and May had ended their partnership.

Pearce had a son named Hosea. When the Civil War broke out, Hosea enlisted as a Confederate soldier. He was captured by Union troops in 1862 and spent the next year or so in a Union prison. In 1863, he was released after he agreed to sign a loyalty oath to the United States government.

At the end of the Civil War, in 1865, Pearce started a tobacco business known as B.C. Pearce, Son and Company in St. Louis. In the 1865 *St. Louis City Directory*, Benjamin C. Pearce and Hosea T. Pearce are listed as the partners of the company, which manufactured smoking tobacco. Pearce also took part in tobacco events, such as the Great St. Louis Tobacco Sale in 1866, and even served as a judge on a committee to determine which tobacco grower produced the best-quality fine-cut tobacco leaves. The event was held at the Pepper Warehouse in St. Louis, considered one of the largest warehouses in the region.

Unfortunately, during this time, Pearce's partnership with his son ended after two years. Due to Hosea's poor health, caused in part by his treatment as a prisoner of war, he sold his interests in the business to his father. Sadly, in early 1867, Hosea died. He was originally buried in St. Louis, but research leads us to believe his wife later had his body moved to Ohio.

By mid- to late 1867, Pearce had begun a new partnership with C.O. and J.N. Evans and established Evans, Pearce and Co., manufactures of fine smoking tobacco. Pearce remained partners with the Evans brothers until May 1868, when he decided to sell his interests in the company. Under the terms of the agreement, the Evans brothers would assume all liabilities and receive all bills and accounts due to the firm.

In late 1869 or early 1870, Pearce went into a partnership with his friend S.W. Logan and refurbished the old mill that Pearce had built around 1858 or 1860, which was located on Mill (Wall) Street. By November 1870, Pearce and Logan were advertising their business in local newspapers. However, before the Pearce and Logan flour mill could become fully operational, Pearce found himself being sued by Robert H. Pendleton on behalf of the heirs of the estate of Henry T. Pendleton, who died in 1871.

The 1870s proved to be financially devastating for Pearce. By March 1871, he was facing massive debt. It appeared that he had signed a promissory note using his real estate property, including his lands, farm and mill, to obtain money to not only build the mill but also to purchase more land from Henry Pendleton in the late 1850s through the 1860s. He and his former partner Pinckney M. May were named as codefendants in the suit and were sued by the heirs of Robert H. Pendleton (deceased) for failure to repay debts. Between 1871 and 1872, real estate property belonging to Pearce was seized by order of the Circuit Court of St. Charles and sold or auctioned off to pay off his debts. As administrator of Robert H. Pendleton's estate, Robert's son Henry T. Pendleton oversaw the liquidation of Pearce's property. Among the property seized was Pearce's Flour Mill, but instead of selling the mill, Henry T. Pendleton reopened it with new equipment. The Peerless Flour Mill operated from 1878 to 1885 until Pendleton, facing his own creditors, was forced to sell the mill in 1887 to John Dirker.

As for Pearce, not only did he suffer financial losses during the 1870s, but he also endured the loss of his wife, Martha, after thirty-six years of marriage in 1876. Perhaps one bright spot came in 1878, when, at the age of sixty-four, he married his second wife, Elizabeth "Betty" Randolph of St. Charles, Missouri.

By 1880, Pearce was living on his farm with his wife, his son Eugene and his daughter-in-law. Pearce was listed as the head of the household in the 1880 federal census, his occupation was that of a laborer. Being near seventy years old, Pearce probably did some general farm jobs on his farm, where he spent his remaining years—although it appears he was still able to be engaged in business and the community during the last few years of his life. In 1881, Pearce was employed by his friend Samuel Grantham as a representative of Grantham's Mercantile Commission in St. Louis, Missouri. In 1882, he was appointed supervisor of road repairs between Wentzville and Flint Hill. However, by then, Pearce's health had been failing for some time, and in the early morning of January 13, 1884, he died at the age of seventy. He was buried at Linn Cemetery in Wentzville, Missouri.

A January 16, 1884 article in the *St. Charles Cosmos* reported that Pearce was "one of the oldest citizens of Wentzville and was at one time said to be well off, being an extensive manufacture of tobacco, but it is presumed, leaves but little property." Within a year of his death, his home and the remaining ninety acres of his farm were put up for sale by J.J. Walker.

Wesley William Sherman

By Lois Kessler
Originally published on the WCHS Facebook page, June 2016

Wesley William Sherman was born on November 27, 1836, in Hickory Grove (a settlement near present-day Warrenton), Warren County, Missouri, to Daniel and Sylvia Paddock Sherman. His father was born in New Hampshire, and his mother was born in New York. Before moving to Warren County, Missouri, Daniel and Sylvia lived with their family in Warren, New York. They moved sometime between 1817 and 1823, and their last four children were born in Warren County. Daniel is buried in the Sherman Family Cemetery in Warren County.

On December 14, 1858, Wesley married Josephine D. Sherman in Flint Hill. Josephine was born in Wentzville on February 27, 1842, to Ira T. and Mary Angeline E. Davis Sherman. Josephine's grandparents David and Margaret Root Sherman are also buried in the Sherman Family Cemetery. It is believed that Wesley and Josephine were cousins of some type. After their marriage, they continued to live in and around Wentzville. County land records of the time show they owned land between Wentzville and Flint Hill. During their marriage, they had eight children, four boys and four girls, all born in Wentzville. Their last son, born in either 1881 or 1883, was named Robert Dula Sherman after the tobacco man Robert Dula of Wentzville.

In the census, Wesley reported his occupation as farmer and tobacconist. The obituary that appeared in the *Wentzville Union* stated: "In Wentzville's early days, Mr. Sherman was one of the town's most prominent and progressive citizens; he was an expert tobacco man and was connected with all of the factories located here before the days of trusts." The paper is referring to a time when there were many small tobacco companies, before they were bought out by bigger firms. So not only did Wesley Sherman and Robert Dula probably work together, but Sherman also probably held Robert Dula in a high regard—thus naming his youngest son in his honor.

Sometime around 1884 or later, the family moved to Montgomery City, where Wesley worked for the Paul Brown Tobacco Company. In 1894, when the company moved to St. Louis, the Sherman family moved with it.

It was reported around the time of the St. Louis World's Fair that Wesley patented a type of portable fence, which he exhibited at several area fairs, but I could find no evidence of this patent.

Sadly, on October 10, 1914, Wesley Sherman took his own life at his home in St. Louis. It is believed he was in ill health and had been for some time. In his obituary, the *Wentzville Union* had this to say:

> He did much in the ways of improving the town; most all the older brick residents were built through his effort. Among them are the Karrenbrock house near the mill (originally the Wentzville Tobacco Factory was built in 1885 and sold at public auction in 1892. Mr. Karrenbrock won the bid and converted the building to a mill) and the house recently sold by N.J. Yahn to Chas. Ruebling.

As you can see, the obituary does not mention his invention of a portable fence. But one also must wonder what his role was in building "brick residents," since he was known as a farmer and then an "expert tobacco man." An interesting side note is that his father-in-law was a carpenter. It's possible he had an interest in the brick factory that used to be on the south side of downtown Wentzville.

The Shermans are buried in Linn Cemetery.

Chapter 4

Medical Professionals of Wentzville

Medical Professionals of Wentzville

By Gerry Matlock
Originally published in the Messenger-Tribune, *September 5 and 12, 1979*

One of the most respected persons in our community was the country doctor. The doctor was the person everyone counted on when they were sick, hurt or were expecting that new arrival and was on the scene regardless of the time or the day of the week and spent countless hours serving others. Now is the time to pay the long overdue tribute to the doctors that they so richly deserve.

In the WCHS Museum, we have a cabinet full of old medical supplies and equipment the doctors used in the 1800s. Some of these supplies/equipment look very intriguing, and I am glad they are not used today! Also located in the cabinet are a medical bag and a prescription label that once belonged to a Dr. Drace.

The early country doctor of the 1800s, according to the book *Small Town*, had to contend with many diseases and plagues that were at times fatal. Cholera and smallpox were highly contagious and could wipe out a community in a very short period.

Flint Hill was almost wiped out by a cholera epidemic about 1845. The worst epidemic of cholera in the county occurred in St. Charles in 1849.

Left: Dr. Drace's medical bag, located in the WCHS Museum. *WCHS Collection.*

Right: Dr. Drace's prescription pad from Wentzville's pharmacy with portfolio cover. *WCHS Collection.*

In 1854, another outbreak occurred. The last great epidemic occurred in 1867. In St. Peter's Cemetery, there is a row of graves known as Cholera Row.

Smallpox was epidemic in the country during several periods, especially during the 1870s. The Klump family of St. Peters were stricken, and all died except one little boy, who did not catch it but carried the disease to others.

Malaria was not generally a killer but lingered on and on. It was common near swamplands, standing water and barnyards, the breeding places of the mosquito.

Chills and dysentery were also very common sicknesses. Dysentery was brought on mostly by eating unripe fruits and drinking water. It was very painful and caused many deaths.

Quinine was the medicine that doctors prescribed most. Many people also resorted to teas from various weeds, roots, barks and leaves to help them.

Some of our first-generation doctors were described in newspaper articles and in the book *History of St. Charles, Warren and Montgomery Counties, Missouri*. This book was written in 1885. Although there were many notable doctors in the area, these are some of the most well known.

William Caldwell, MD

By Gerry Matlock
Originally published in the Messenger-Tribune, *September 5 and 12, 1979*
Updates added by Lois Kessler

Dr. Caldwell was born on October 14, 1871, in Warrick County, Indiana. He practiced medicine in Wentzville from May 1929 until his death in 1937.

In 1903, Dr. Caldwell married Carrie Wilson from Essex, Missouri. They had three children: Jerry, Reginald and Wilma. During this time, Dr. Caldwell practiced medicine in Stoddard County for many years.

In 1928, Dr. Caldwell came to St. Charles County and lived in Howell, Missouri. In May 1929, he moved to Wentzville and opened his practice in the Wullschleger Building. He and his wife lived upstairs, while his medical offices were on the first floor. The Wullschleger Building was located at 8 West Main Street and has since been torn down.

In 1934 or 1935, Gus Temme bought the Wullschleger building, at which time the building became known as the Temme Building. Dr. Caldwell moved his practice and family to the Eliza Dierker home on South Main Street. It is believed that this home sat on the southwest corner of Elm Street and South Main Street.

Dr. Caldwell was a member of the Christian Church, the American Medical Association, the Masonic Order and the Odd Fellows. After his death on February 15, 1937, and funeral in Wentzville, his body was transported to Essex, Missouri, for burial.

Joseph Goodrich, DDS

By Lois Kessler
Originally published on the WCHS Facebook page, January 23, 2017

Dr. Goodrich was a dentist in Wentzville for over forty years. He was born in Amherst County, Virginia, on April 14, 1825, to Gideon (1785–1835) and Elizabeth Carter (1793–1859) Goodrich. A biography of the dentist indicates that the family was of Welsh descent and had been in America since the 1700s or before. Dr. Goodrich's grandfather Edmund and great-grandfather Thomas moved from Carolina County to Amherst County, Virginia, in the year 1732.

In 1830, the family moved west to Missouri and settled in Callaway County and, later, in Monroe County. His father was a farmer, and Dr. Goodrich received his early education in the small schools in Callaway and Monroe Counties and from his father.

In 1847, Dr. Goodrich enlisted in the United States Army. The enlistment was for five years. He fought in the Mexican-American War, and in July 1848, he received an honorable discharge with a government pension. Joseph returned to the family farm and remained there for the next two years.

Dr. Goodrich trained in what was then called the dental arts under Dr. Socrates Hubbard in Danville, Missouri. Dr. Hubbard was a physician who had come to Missouri from the East and had "on occasion" practiced dentistry. After training for less than three months, Dr. Goodrich opened a dental practice in Danville, Missouri, in 1852.

In 1858, he married Ann Sarah Frans (born October 27, 1835), in Truxton, Missouri. Both families were from Virginia; Ann's mother was a Shelton, and her grandmother was an Allen, early settlers in the Wentzville area.

In 1859, Dr. Goodrich and Ann settled in Wentzville. Ann's parents, William and Nancy Shelton Frans, lived with them. In fact, throughout their married lives, Ann's parents lived with the family, and the 1880 census shows that even though Ann had passed away and his son-in-law Dr. Goodrich had remarried, William Frans continued to live with Dr. Goodrich. Dr. Goodrich and Ann had eight children: Carrie, who married Melville S. Ball; Mary, who married Preston Randolph; John J., who married Mary Ingersall; Anna, who was born around 1865 and died sometime before 1880; Nancy, who married William S. Heady Jr.; Joseph Jr., who was born in 1869 and died in 1872; William, who married Louise Sloat and also became a dentist; and James, their last child. Ann Frans Goodrich died on September 28, 1875, and was buried in Linn Cemetery.

On August 10, 1879, Dr. Goodrich married Mrs. Maria Julia Womack. Maria commonly used various forms of her first name (Marie, Mary and Mariah) and also frequently used Julia as her first name. Mrs. Womack's maiden name was Duncan; her father was Carey Duncan from Moscow Mills, Missouri. I believe that the marriage to Dr. Goodrich was her third. She first married Samuel Abington on February 28, 1855, and had two children: a daughter, Flora (who married Purl Parker), and a son, William B. Abington. On September 28, 1865, Maria, using the name Julia M. Abington, married Thomas T. Womack. She brought to this marriage her two children and her mother. The Womacks had one daughter, Julia. This daughter, Julia Womack, would marry Caleb C. Dula, who became president and later chairman of the board of Ligget and Myers Tobacco Company. The 1880 census shows Julia/Mary's son William B. Abington living with the Goodrich family. Williams's occupation is listed as dental student. In fact, William Abington would later be a dentist in St. Louis, Missouri. Maria Julia Duncan Abington Womack Goodrich died on July 29, 1897. Maria was originally buried in Linn Cemetery in Wentzville, Missouri. In 1925, her body was moved to the Dula-Wightman Mausoleum at the Sleepy Hollow Cemetery in Westchester County, New York. She is interred with both her daughters.

Dr. Goodrich practiced dentistry in Wentzville and surrounding towns for forty years. He frequently advertised in the Troy paper and often entered partnerships with other dentists. One such partner was William Abington, his stepson. It was reported that in 1857, he made a full set of teeth, which were the first made in Montgomery, Warren and Lincoln Counties. One account I read said that "he possessed exceptional skills as a gold foil operator and in prosthetic work." This article went on to describe Dr. Goodrich as "a man of great energy, well informed in professional matters, and ranked among the most prominent members of the [dental] fraternity throughout the state." He was a charter member of the Missouri State Dental Association (MSDA). When he began the study of the dental profession, it was crude at best, but Dr. Goodrich is credited with developing new ideas and plans that were adopted by others in the profession. In 1870, he was elected president of the MSDA. In 1890, the Missouri Dental College conferred upon him an honorary DDS degree.

In addition to being a dentist, Dr. Goodrich was also involved in other businesses. From 1863 through 1876, he was in the tobacco business. Around 1869, he entered a partnership with Joel Carr to manufacture tobacco products under the firm name of Carr, Johnson and Company. Within a year Carr bought out the doctor's shares and partnered with Robert B. Dula. Carr and Goodrich would partner again between the years 1885 and 1887 in the hardware business.

In December 1898, Wentzville had a fire that destroyed an entire block of the business district. The *Warrenton Banner* reported, "The fire was discovered in the wagon shop of F. Schierbaum and spread to an immense warehouse and a large boarding house occupied by Mrs. Boyd." This house also included the offices of the *Wentzville Union* and Dr. Goodrich, and the *Banner* article referred to it as the Goodrich Building. The *Banner* reported that all buildings were of frame construction and "burned like kindling wood." Loses were estimated at $10,000, and the owners only carried about $4,000 in insurance. The *Banner* expected all buildings to be rebuilt. Later that month, the *Banner* reported that Dr. Goodrich had sustained a "considerable loss" and he had disposed of his real estate and was going to retire and move to Chillicothe, Missouri, to live with his son William, who was also a dentist.

Dr. Goodrich never moved to Chillicothe, based on minutes from the Masonic Lodge. Dr. Goodrich was a thirty-two-year member of the Masonic Fraternity. From the lodge minutes of November 11, 1899: "Bro J. C. Goodrich was reported as sick."

Dr. Goodrich passed away on November 29, 1899, the Wednesday before Thanksgiving. He was laid to rest on Thanksgiving Day. His obituary notes that the Masonic Lodge oversaw the funeral arrangements. Dr. Goodrich is buried in Linn Cemetery with his first wife.

James David Harris, MD, and Family

By Lois Kessler
Originally published on the WCHS Facebook page, March 1, 2018

A blinding snow fell on January 8, 1886, in Wentzville. The St. Louis train from Omaha, which did not stop in Wentzville, was running three hours late. Dr. James D. Harris was a respected doctor and druggist in Wentzville. Even though he was only in his forties, he was also very hard of hearing, maybe even deaf. When he decided to cross the railroad tracks, he thought the train had already been through town, and blinded by the snow and hard of hearing, he stepped directly in front of the oncoming train. His body was thrown onto the platform of the train station, where he breathed his last. When he died, Dr. Harris left a widow, Sarah, and two children, Claudia and Warren Savage Harris. Dr. Harris is buried at Linn Cemetery in Wentzville.

In my research, I have been able to find very little about Dr. Harris. It is believed he was born in 1842, possibly in Wentzville or on the family farm just outside of town after his parents and two older sisters come to the area from Virginia around 1840. The 1870 census shows Dr. Harris living in Wentzville with an older man named William Harris. Probate records for William show that he was Dr. Harris's uncle. The same records show that James's father was Rueben Harris. Rueben was married to Prudence Harris. It is thought they were cousins, but whether they were first cousins or more distantly related is unknown. James David was their youngest child. His two older sisters, Martha and Mary, married brothers David and Edward Richards.

Rueben, Prudence, Martha, Mary and the Richards brothers are buried in the Richards Farm Cemetery off North Point Prairie Road.

It is not known how James Harris received his training. A common practice during this time was for a person to train under a doctor without receiving what we now call a formal education. It is also possible that James studied at a college here in Missouri or in Virginia.

On April 1, 1873, Dr. Harris married Sarah Ward Savage. Sarah was born on August 30, 1854, in Wentzville, the middle daughter of Joseph Warren and Ruth Mattie Keithly Savage. Her father was a surveyor and involved in the tobacco industry in Wentzville. It was said that Mr. Savage was one of the first to recognize the possibilities of Wentzville and moved his family to the town shortly after the original survey, although they had lived in the area before moving to Wentzville proper.

Warren passed away in 1893 when he was about eleven and was buried in Linn Cemetery with his father. On December 15, 1895, the *St. Louis Post Dispatch* ran a feature titled "Society Belles of Wentzville," and Claudia Harris was one of the featured belles. The article describes her as follows: "Her features are perfect, she has dark hair, brown eyes, very fair complexion and is of medium height." It goes on to say that she is a "graduate of instrumental and vocal music of St. Louis and St. Charles" but does not mention any school. She was an organist at the Methodist church and was said to have an excellent voice.

The article must have worked, because in 1896, she married Robert Akeman May, a lawyer. Robert's father was Robert F. May. The Mays were early settlers in Wentzville, and Robert F. May was a large landowner. May Road is named after the family, and May family descendants still live in Wentzville. Several May family members moved from Wentzville to Louisiana, Missouri, including Robert and Claudia; they reportedly had a son and daughter.

Sarah followed her daughter and, sometime around 1900, married Thomas Lilburn May, a widower who was her son-in-law's uncle. On July 21, 1920, Thomas was struck by a train and died a day and a half later of his injuries. For the second time in her life, Sarah was a widow—both husbands having been killed when hit by a train. Thomas is buried in Riverview Cemetery in Louisiana, Missouri, with his first wife.

Robert and Claudia divorced sometime before 1923. Claudia and Sarah would continue to live in Louisiana, Missouri. When Sara died on July

19, 1929, she was buried in Linn Cemetery next to her husband and son. Claudia would remain in Louisiana until her death on October 7, 1941. She is buried in Linn Cemetery next to her mother, father and brother.

William August Heinritz, MD

By Lois Kessler

Dr. Heinritz was born on March 20, 1877, in Wright City, Missouri, the son of Christian and Margaret Schmidt Heinritz. He graduated from the Marion-Sims-Beaumont Dental College in St. Louis in 1903. The college was located on the southeast corner of Grand Avenue and Caroline Street. It was purchased by St. Louis University in 1903. Dr. Heinritz practiced as a dentist until his death.

According to the 1910 and 1920 censuses, he owned a home on South Main. It appears the home was located next door, on the east side of the Musick home. In the 1930s, the census listed him as a renter. It was about

Residence of Dr. W.R. Heinritz in Wentzville. *WCHS Collection.*

this time that his wife, who suffered from some type of lung ailment, started spending part of the year living in Denver, Colorado. It was also during this time that Dr. Heinritz started buying farm property and leasing the land.

Dr. Heinritz was found dead on March 27, 1939, in a field on a farm he owned in Black Walnut, slumped over the steering wheel of his car. The death certificate lists the cause as apoplexy. After his death, his wife remained in Colorado. She died in 1955. They are both buried in Linn Cemetery.

John A. Talley, MD

By Gerry Matlock
Originally published in the Messenger-Tribune*, September 12, 1979*
Updates and further research added by Lois Kessler

Dr. John A. Talley, for many years, engaged in the practice of medicine and surgery in Wentzville. He was born on July 5, 1813, in Cumberland, Virginia, the son of William P. and Frances (Daniel) Talley. He received his early education in local private schools and was proficient in Greek and Latin. At the age of seventeen, he was sent to Randolph and Macon College, where he concluded his general education. While at Randolph and Macon College, he decided he wanted to enter into the medical profession, and at the age of nineteen, he preceptored under his older brother, Dr. Zach Talley. In September 1839, he entered the medical department of the University of Virginia. In July 1840, he graduated with honors in medicine and surgery. His first job out of college was as the assistant surgeon at the almshouse in Richmond, Virginia. He soon left the almshouse and went into practice with his brother. In the winters of 1840–41 and 1841–42, he took postgraduate courses at Virginia Medical College. In 1842, believing that there would be more opportunities in the West, he started on horseback for Missouri, followed by his favorite pointer dog. He arrived in St. Charles County in November 1842, where he took up residence with the Colonel C.F. Woodson family, who resided a few miles south of Wentzville. He soon built up a large practice. "During the sickly season of 1844, he was kept so constantly in the saddle that he could not procure the proper amount of rest and came near sacrificing his own life in his efforts to save others."

On March 27, 1845, in St. Charles, Missouri, he married Pauline C. Preston from Montogomery County, Virginia, a daughter of Colonel

W.R. Preston. The Preston family was one of the most distinguished and extensive in the United States. Pauline's family boasted statesmen, soldiers and scholars.

Dr. John A. Talley started practicing medicine in the 1840s in Wentzville. *WCHS Collection.*

John Talley was a Democrat, and in 1853, he was nominated and elected to the Missouri legislature, where he served the people with marked ability and public fidelity. After serving one term, he refused to be renominated, as he felt it would interfere with his medical practice. He was also one of the active men in the county in forwarding the building of the North Missouri Railroad and was one of the prominent directors of the company.

The doctor's restless energy caused him to make a change, and he entered extensively into the manufacturing and banking businesses in the town of St. Charles, belonging to firms known as Paule and Talley, and Griffith and Talley. He also served as director of the First National Bank of St. Charles. He also went largely into land speculations. He made money very rapidly, but at the same time, his generosity and unsuspicious character caused him to suffer serious losses. As a result of the Civil War and debts, he lost property and money to the amount of over $6,000.

Dr. Talley did not allow these misfortunes to dishearten him. In 1865, he opened an office in Wentzville, and he again cheerfully turned to his profession and soon built up once more a splendid business. This increased steadily until 1875, when he served an unparalleled number of between three hundred and four hundred families. He was assisted by his son Dr. W.P. Talley.

He was a very powerful surgeon and performed in this neighborhood some of the most important and intricate surgical operations with perfect success. One example was an Irishman named Jerry Sullivan, a railroad man, that was knocked down at Wentzville by a freight car, one wheel of which passed over his thigh, mangling and smashing it almost off. Dr. Talley, against the advice of his colleagues, insisted on amputating the limb and thus saved the man's life.

Some accounts say that the doctor and his wife were blessed with five children, but further research leads us to believe they only had two sons:

Wentzville home of Dr. John Talley, pictured here with his family in the front yard. *WCHS Collection.*

William P. and Edwin P. Both sons became doctors. Edwin would die at the age of thirty-four in New Mexico from consumption, leaving a wife and two young children.

Dr. Talley owned valuable property in town—in fact, the family home was located on Talley Street in Wentzville, and the street is named after the family. He was a member of the Masonic order for over fifty years.

Dr. Talley passed away on September 10, 1885. He had practiced medicine in Wentzville for more than forty years. It was reported that he was one of the oldest and most successful physicians of St. Charles County. Paulina passed away in 1886, and they are both buried in South Linn Cemetery.

William P. Talley, MD

By Gerry Matlock
Originally published in the Messenger-Tribune, *September 12, 1979*
Updates and further research added by Lois Kessler

William P. Talley was a son of Dr. John A. Talley and was born in St. Charles County in 1846. He early displayed a taste for studies of a medical character and, while yet a youth, decided to devote himself to the profession of medicine. He was educated with that object in view and took a course at St. Charles College. Immediately after completing his college course, he began the regular study of medicine under his father and later attended the medical department at the State University of Virginia. He graduated with honors in the class of 1868.

He took a postgraduate course at the St. Louis Medical College and received a diploma of graduation. In 1869, he began the practice of medicine in this county. He soon established himself in the confidence of the public and acquired a good practice. In 1874, he married Miss Lucy Preston Talley of Mississippi, a distant relative. They had four children: Joseph H. (1876–1950), who became a doctor; Martha (1878–1882); Goldie (1887–1958), who became a RN, and Pauline (born in 1883), who died as a child.

Horace Alfred Talley, MD

By Lois Kessler

Dr. Horace Alfred Talley was born in Virginia on August 20, 1863. His family had a long history of being medical doctors. He received his early education in Virginia and settled in Wentzville around 1885 to practice medicine with his uncle, Dr. John Talley, the first physician and surgeon of Wentzville.

On August 19, 1888, the day before his birthday, Dr. Tally married Laura Dierker (1865–1915). Her mother was Eliza Michel Dierker (1844–1936), and her father was Ernst H. Dierker (1834–1883). Her brother was Sheriff John H. Dierker. The Talleys had three children: Ernest (1889–1964; married Emma Rau), Horace (1892–1942) and Vara (1894–1991; married Arthur Mudd and Webster F. Karrenbrock).

At the peak of his practice, he was endeared by numberless patients and was considered almost to be "family" in most of the homes he visited. Dr. Talley was elected mayor of Wentzville in 1896 and again in 1902 and was instrumental in helping Wentzville attain the designation of a fourth-class city in 1903.

Around 1909, the Talley family moved to Santa Anna, California, and then Orange County, California. Many of Laura's Dierker relatives had previously moved to the area, and the move may have been prompted by Laura's health. While in California, Dr. Talley did not practice medicine but was involved in real estate, buying and selling property. In 1912, they were preparing to build a home in Los Angeles to be near Vara, who was in school there. While the Talleys were preparing to visit Vara in Los Angeles, Laura

Left: Dr. Horace Alfred Talley was the nephew of Dr. John Talley and came to Wentzville in the 1890s to practice medicine with his uncle. *WCHS Collection.*

Right: Dr. Horace Talley's wife, Laura Dierker, when she was young. *WCHS Collection.*

accidently shot herself in the right temple. The papers reported the accident and said she had tried to commit suicide and was "temporarily deranged mentally." Laura and the family all said that it was an accident and she was not suicidal. The papers retracted their statement, and Laura recovered.

Sometime in 1913, Dr. Talley returned to Wentzville, and in January 1914, he reopened his practice. It is unclear if Laura and Vara came with him. The boys, now young men, stayed in California. It is possible that Laura was spending winters in California and then the rest of the year in Wentzville. What is known is that in January 1915, Laura was in California and Vara and Dr. Talley were in Wentzville, expecting her to join them in the spring, when they got word that Laura was ill. Vara returned to California to tend to her mother. In April, word reached Wentzville that Laura was dying. Her mother immediately left for California, but unfortunately, she arrived in California two hours after her daughter passed away. It is unclear if Dr. Talley was in California or if he returned for his wife's burial.

On January 30, while responding to the Schierbaum Blacksmith Shop to dress the wounded hand of William Kleimeier, Dr. Horace Talley was crossing the railroad tracks at the Karrenbrock Crossing (we are unsure

Dr. Horace Talley's home in Wentzville. *WCHS Collection.*

where this crossing was located) when his Ford Runabout was struck by Wabash passenger train no. 20 and he passed away at the young age of fifty-four. Dr. Talley had recently purchased the car. On this day, he had a problem starting the car, and a man working in a yard near his vehicle helped him. As Dr. Talley neared the tracks, the man noticed that a train was approaching and shouted out to Dr. Talley. But Dr. Talley did not hear the warning. It is interesting to note that a few days before his accident, his daughter Vara had driven the car, had trouble with the steering and ended up running the car into a tree. The car was not damaged in Vara's accident, and it was thought that the steering problem had been repaired.

Dr. Talley was a thirty-second degree Mason at the time of passing, and the Masonic Lodge took care of the funeral. He is buried in South Linn Cemetery near his uncle.

Chapter 5

Women of Wentzville, 1855 to the Early 1900s

Catherine A. Thompson

By Kathy Weindel, August 2023

Catherine Ann Thompson was born on June 28, 1838, on her parents' farm in Wentzville. Her parents were Walter and Mary Thompson, and in the early 1830s, they came to Wentzville, Missouri, from Virginia. Catherine grew up on the family farm with her brothers, John and Thomas, and her sisters, Cornelia and Mary.

In 1854, when Catherine's mother, Mary Thompson, passed, Catherine and her sisters, Cornelia and Mary, took over the responsibilities of running the household while the two brothers, John and Thomas, helped their father, Walter, with the farming.

In 1861, the Civil War began, and the two brothers went off to fight in the war. When it was over, they returned home and helped their father again with the farm.

A few years after the Civil War ended, the brothers decided to leave the family farm and do something different. Thomas still wanted to farm but not on the family farm, so he purchased land in Warren County, married a local girl and raised a family on his farm. John wanted to become a tobacco merchant and businessman. In 1867, he convinced the family to build a hotel in Wentzville. By 1868, the building had been built, but it was not used as a hotel. Instead, John decided it would be named the Thompson

The old three-story Thompson building where the Thompson sisters worked is on the far right. *WCHS Collection.*

Building and used for offices, businesses and shops. John reasoned that an office building would bring new businesses to Wentzville and it would help the town grow and prosper. John was the first to open his business in the Thompson Building, as a tobacco merchant.

At this time, the Thompson Building was ready for more tenants. The father, Walter, and one sister, Mary, had passed. John insisted that his two sisters still living, Cornelia and Catherine, leave the farm and live with him in Wentzville. Cornelia and Catherine assumed that they would become the housekeepers of his home. But John was concerned for his two sisters and their future. He wanted them to take up a profession that would provide them with a livelihood and independence and give him peace of mind.

So Catherine and Cornelia decided to open a dressmaking and millinery shop in the Thompson Building in the early 1880s. They worked hard to make their business successful. They had to become aware of and study the latest fashions. For their customers, they purchased magazines and catalogs showing the latest dress and hat styles. In the 1880s, they made bustle dresses, and in 1895, they started adding mutton sleeves to shirtwaists and dresses. During the late 1800s, daytime dresses were made of cotton, muslin or wool.

The colors for daytime dresses were blue, green or purple. Evening wear required silk, satin and lace in black, red or ivory.

Catherine and Cornelia became skilled in doing proper fittings by carefully taking their clients' measurements and recording them in a notebook. They also had to know how to use sewing patterns, a sewing machine and how to hand sew the finest stitches. They learned how to purchase fabric and sewing supplies and how to deal with vendors and wholesale companies. They became expert in serving their customers and accommodating them to the best of their abilities.

By working hard over the years, they made their shop successful. However, there were a few times when they thought they were going to lose their business.

Their brother John had been managing the Thompson Building, but when he died from a heart attack in 1898, their remaining brother, Thomas, wanted to sell the building. Catherine persuaded him not to sell. Then

DAR women in 1903 wearing clothes and hats similar to those Catherine Thompson and her sister Cornelia made. *DAR Collection (S0204); SHSMO-Columbia.*

Catherine became the building manager, taking on new responsibilities such as collecting rent from tenants, having repairs done and renting out rooms for town events like dances.

Another time they nearly lost the building was in 1906, when a fire broke out in a livery stable behind it. Thankfully, the fire was put out, and their business and the Thompson Building were saved.

The years went by quickly, but Catherine and Cornelia still enjoyed being dressmakers and milliners. In 1910, they both retired as dressmakers and milliners, but Catherine continued as manager of the Thompson Building. In 1922, Cornelia passed, and on March 20, 1923, Catherine passed at the age of eighty-four. Both of their services were held at the family home, and both were laid to rest in Linn Cemetery with their family.

Virginia (Jenni) Lee Johnson Clark

By Kathy Weindel, August 2023

Virginia was born in March 1864 on a family farm in an area called Oak Dale near Wentzville. Her parents were George and Margaret Johnson. She spent her childhood growing up on the family farm, where there were always chores to be done. Fortunately, her father had plenty of farmhands, as he and her mother had a total of seventeen children.

Besides working on the farm, Jenni was able to attend the local one-room school, where she could enjoy making friends and learning to read and write. She enjoyed writing the most of all her classes. Her friends thought that she would become a fine writer.

In 1887, at the age of twenty-two, Jenni thought she would have to spend the rest of her life on the farm, dependent on her family for financial support. But then, in 1888, she was offered an opportunity for a career that was not normally open to women. Jenni was offered the position of postmistress for Wentzville. She thought that, in part, what helped her to be offered such a position was her friendly personality, her work ethic and being from a well-respected family. By accepting the appointment, she became the first female postmaster, or postmistress, of Wentzville, Missouri. On July 7, 1888, she was officially appointed postmaster, as the previous postmaster had died at seventy-seven years old.

Once she received her appointment, Jenni had to take an oath of office, supply a bond (which was good faith money) and obtain references from two upstanding members of the community. These three things were required in case she violated her oath of loyalty or stole money from the post office. She then received her commission and began her duties as postmistress.

When she began as postmistress in 1887, the post office was in the Thompson Building, which was managed by her friend Miss Catherine Thompson.

As postmistress, Jenni had certain responsibilities, and the first thing she had to do was take an inventory of post office property and the mail. She had to appoint an assistant postmaster in case she had to travel or was ill and not able to work, and she chose John Bornhop, who would be a most dependable assistant.

Jenni also had to keep the post office open from Monday through Friday. If the post office had to be open on Sunday because mail needed to be sorted, she had to wait to open until after church services.

Unfortunately, there was no rural mail service, so folks had to come to the post office to mail their letters or parcels as well as pick up their mail. At the time, the cost of postage stamps was based on the weight of the item. The cost was two cents per ounce, and Jenni's salary was based on how much money was made from selling postage stamps per quarter.

Throughout the year, Jenni had other responsibilities. She had to prepare a quarterly report for the postmaster general, which included types of mail sent and received, monies received for postage and expenses paid (one example is rent).

Sadly, during Jenni's time as postmistress, she sometimes had to deal with health issues that prevented her from working. During those times, she was thankful that she had John Bornhop as her assistant, as he was very capable of managing the post office. By 1897, Jenni realized that she needed to resign as postmistress as her health was not improving and she was spending less time at the post office. And so she resigned.

Jenni recommended John Bornhop for the position of postmaster following her resignation, and in 1898, he applied and was accepted as the next postmaster.

After Jenni resigned as postmistress, she returned to her family's farm. With the help of family and friends, her health did improve. She was even well enough to take a trip to Nashville, Tennessee, to visit relatives.

By the time she had left the post office, she was thirty-three years old, and marriage looked very unlikely. But then, in 1908, she did marry. Jenni met and married Benjamin (Ben) Clark. After they married, she moved to his home in Iowa. Then, in 1920, they moved to Lamar, Missouri, where they planned to live out their lives on a small farm. They never had any children, but they did have many nieces and nephews.

One fond memory Jenni cherished was spending time with her relatives at the Johnson family reunion in the summer of 1927. They had such a wonderful time telling stories about their childhoods, each of her brothers and sisters trying to outdo the others' stories. It was nice to see so many of her siblings after so many years. Many of them had traveled from California, Michigan and different parts of Missouri.

In 1935, Jenni's health was growing worse, so she and Ben moved into her sister Mary's home in St. Louis. Mary had always been the caretaker of the family, and she took care of Jenni.

On a Tuesday morning in April 1936, Jenni passed at the age of seventy-two. The following Wednesday evening, the service was held at a chapel on Lindell Boulevard near her sister's home. Jenni was buried at Linn Cemetery on Thursday afternoon after a short service.

Mary Louise Dalton

By Lois Kessler, August 2022

Mary Louise Dalton was the daughter of Dr. William R.I. Dalton and Harriet Ursula Walker Dalton. She was born on April 1, 1869, in her grandparents' home in Wentzville, the same home where her mother and probably most of her Walker aunts and uncles were born. Her grandparents were Warren and Mary Baker May Walker. Warren and Mary were early settlers in the area, having come from Rockingham County, North Carolina, in 1830. I believe their home, which they called Cedar Grove, was somewhere between Wilmer Road and Heppermann Road. While I have not researched the land claims in this area, I base this assumption on the location of the Warren Walker Cemetery.

Mary Louise's ancestors on both her maternal and paternal side fought in the War of 1776, the War of 1812 and the Civil War. Her paternal grandfather, Dr. Robert Hunter Dalton, was a surgeon in the Confederate army, as was her father. Her maternal grandfather, Charles Powahatan May, fought with Andrew Jackson in the Seminole War, and her maternal uncle Benjamin F. Walker was with General Price in the Confederate army. It is interesting to note how attitudes about which side one fought on during the Civil War have changed over the years. In the book *History of St. Louis, Vol. 1*, published in 1899, when discussing the Dalton family's participation in the Civil War on the Confederate side, the authors state, "These facts bear evidence to the chivalrous character of the family to which Miss Dalton belongs."

Mary Louise was an educated woman. She attended the Rockingham School, and from there she went to the Pritchett School, also known as the Paynesville Preparatory School, in Paynesville, Missouri. After graduating from Pritchett, she went on to Lindenwood College in St. Charles. Her junior year at Lindenwood, she won a $260 scholarship prize, and she graduated with honors in 1887. After Lindenwood, she attended a private school in New York City and learned stenography. After leaving school, she worked as a stenographer in a law office in New York, and a few years later, she moved to Middlesboro, Kentucky, and worked at a bank. Remember, this was during an era when most women did not work outside the home.

Around 1893, Mary Louise moved to St. Louis, Missouri, and went to work for the *Republic*. She wrote book reviews and other articles, eventually becoming the editor of their Sunday magazine. Around 1898 or as late as 1901, she left her job at the *Republic* and moved to Colorado for her health. Based on different accounts I have seen, she may have suffered from typhoid or malaria. After being in Colorado for a couple of months, she returned home to Wentzville to finish recuperating. Her stay in Wentzville lasted two years, during which time she became immersed in genealogy and the history of the region. At the end of the two years, she moved to Jefferson City, Missouri, and became the private secretary of her uncle Charles J. Walker, who was a state senator. I have also read that she deliberately picked Jefferson City because it allowed her to continue her historical research.

In 1903, she became the librarian of the Missouri Historical Society (today, most of us call the Missouri Historical Society the Missouri History Museum, located in the area of the St. Louis Zoo). Her job during this time was to help prepare the society's exhibit for the 1904 St. Louis World's Fair. It was the largest historical exhibit at the fair. In recognition of her efforts, the exposition awarded her a silver or gold medal as a "Collaborator of History." Accounts differ as to whether the medal was silver or gold, and it is quite possible that she was awarded two medals.

During the 1905 session of the state legislature, it is said that Mary had more to do than anyone else to secure the passage of the "Flag Bill," by visiting with every member of the legislature in Jefferson City. The Flag

Mary Louise Dalton, in 1905, secured the passage of the Flag Bill by visiting every member of the Missouri legislature. *Courtesy of Missouri Historical Society, Identifier N22883.*

Bill prohibits the commercial desecration of the American flag and provides for the annual celebration of Flag Day on June 14.

Sadly, Mary Louise Dalton died on June 13, 1907, from an ear infection that, without antibiotics, turned into cerebral meningitis. She was living with her mother at 6003A Maple Avenue in St. Louis. At the time of her death, she was internationally known, regarded as a leading Missouri authority on early French and Spanish settlements in the area. The historical society credited her with "service of immeasurable worth." It was reported that she often traveled throughout the state rescuing historical records that lay hidden in odd places and were on the verge of destruction. Shortly before her death, she had traveled to New Orleans, Louisiana, to study records there. After her death, writeups about Mary Louise described her as "endowed with a keen and alert mind," "quick to perceive relations and values on the materials of history," "indefatigable in her pursuit of historical documents," "a person of decided opinions," a woman with "a passion for accuracy" whose "friendships drew no lines of creed or class," "unfailing cheerful" and "refined, courteous, gentle respectful and generous." In a letter to the society, Miss Mary Simonds of the St. Louis Mercantile Library described traveling with her to ferret out information and had this to say about those trips: "Her way of enlisting the attention, the confidence and finally the enthusiasm of the people we met in these excursions was a constant delight to witness."

Mary Louise Dalton was the founder of the Jefferson Chapter of the DAR and of the Daughters of the Confederacy and a member of the Folk Lore Society and the Confederate Memorial Monument Association.

A funeral service was held for her in St. Louis, and then her body was brought by train to Wentzville, where a second service was held at the Methodist Church. She was buried on Flag Day, June 14, 1907, in Linn Cemetery. She was survived by her mother in Missouri; her father, who was living in Washington State; and her brother Warren Dalton Sr.

Mamie Dierker Ball

By Lois Kessler, August 2024

Mamie Dierker Ball (*pictured*) and eight other ladies were called the "Belles of Wentzville" and said to have "pleasing forms and faces, modesty, conduct and graces." *WCHS Collection.*

Maria "Mamie" Henrietta Dierker Ball was born on February 24, 1875, and died on May 15, 1970. She was born in the Northside Hotel, also known as the Wentzville Hotel, later the Heady Hotel. She was known as Mamie or Mayme. She spent her ninety-five years living in Wentzville. Her father, George Dierker, built the Wentzville Hotel in 1867; it stood on the corner of West Allen and Linn Avenue until it was torn down in 1972. She was the third daughter of George Casper Dierker and Henrietta Mathilde Peters Dierker. Her father was born at sea in 1842 on the ship *Agnes*, while his parents were immigrating to the United States. Her maternal grandfather was Rudolph Peters. Rudolph was involved in various businesses in Wentzville and St. Louis.

Mamie was a graduate of the Synodical College in Fulton, Missouri (a two-year college), where she majored in "piano and organ, and literary and music." In 1895, she was featured in the *St. Louis Post Dispatch* as one of the "society belles of Wentzville." The article describes her as a "splendid entertainer" and a graceful young woman, with dark hair and eyes and a fine singing voice. I remember Mamie as being tall and thin. The article also stated that she had wealthy family connections. Her grandfather was well off, and it is also possible that her grandfather and an uncle were connected with the Peters Shoe Company, which later became the International Shoe Company.

In 1901, Wentzville Presbyterian organized a Sunday school, and Mamie was the secretary. She also served as the organist for the church for thirty years.

On April 27, 1903, she married Marshall "Marsh" E. Ball. Marsh was thirty-seven; Mamie was twenty-eight. Marsh was born in Wentzville in 1865. When they got married, Marsh had a livery stable and operated a transfer business called Ball Transfer. In 1908, before there was Pitman Funeral Home in Wentzville, Marsh entered the funeral business. He was affiliated with Keithly Funeral in O'Fallon. In the early 1900s, he also sold and shipped Christmas trees to St. Louis and other areas.

The Balls lived on Wall Street. Mamie's parents also had a splendid home on Wall. In July 1915, a cyclone (tornado) came through Wentzville and destroyed her parents' home. Pictures and paperwork from her parents' home were discovered in Alton and Alhambra, Illinois. On July 11, the *Post Dispatch* ran a picture of a small child accompanying the story of how a Mrs. Waldo Fisher of the Alton, Illinois area had found the picture in her garden. Mrs. Fisher hoped someone would recognize the photo and she could return it to its rightful owner. Mamie saw the photo and wrote to Mrs. Fisher. In her letter, Mamie explained that the Wentzville home of her mother, Henrietta Peters Dierker, had been destroyed in the tornado. The photo was of Mamie as a toddler and had been part of an album her mother had made. The picture had traveled some forty miles during the cyclone. Another similar story goes that on July 16, 1915, James Tabor, while stacking wheat in his field in Alhambra, Illinois, found a promissory note for $6.05 dated April 18, 1876, payable to Mamie's father, George Dierker. Alhambra, Illinois, is seventy miles from Wentzville.

When Mamie died in 1970, she had been a widow for thirty-seven years. She and Marshall are buried in South Linn Cemetery.

Society Belles of Wentzville: Pleasing Forms and Faces, Modesty, Conduct, Graces

Compiled by Gerry Matlock

Authors' note: "Society Belles of Wentzville" was originally published in the St. Louis Post Dispatch on December 12, 1895, and again in the *Wentzville Union* in 1934. This article, compiled by Gerry Matlock, was published in the *Wentzville Union* on July 9, 1975.

Many have been the groups of fair faces that have adorned the pages of the Sunday Post Dispatch from time to time as belles of Missouri towns, but no town is more favored in the possession of lovely girls than is Wentzville. During the 1890s, towns would select young ladies as "belles" of their towns, and pictures and descriptions of the belles would be published in local and St. Louis papers.

In filial love and obedience, in modesty and energy, in cheerfulness and possession of many Christian virtues, the Wentzville girl (belle) may bid defiance of the slings and arrows of meaner minds, for with these heart ornaments they stand aloof and aloft, clad in the true riches of character. In the December 12, 1895 edition of the *St. Louis Post-Dispatch*, an article appeared with pictures of five and descriptions of nine "Wentzville belles":

Miss Minnie Walker is the daughter of W.W. Walker, a prominent businessman of this town, and is a sister to Ed S. Walker, a member of the firm of Allen and Walker, general merchants. She has light hair, blue eyes, fair complexion, is very popular, and was educated at Fayette College.

Miss Eugenia Harlow is the daughter of Hon. R.J. Harlow of Charleston, Miss., who makes her home with her uncle, Dr. J.T. Evans. She is a handsome and graceful blue-eyed blond, very modest; was educated in the best schools of the South; and is a typical Southern beauty with a large circle of admiring friends.

Miss Lillie Carr is the daughter of the late Thomas Carr, a relative of R.B. Dula, tobacconist of St. Louis. She has dark hair, black eyes, lovely features and complexion, and is a good singer. She has winning ways and is popular.

Miss Lizzie Wullschleger and Miss Edith Wullschleger are the daughters of F. Wullschleger, a prominent and successful hardware dealer. Lizzie is a decided brunette, with dark hair and eyes, fine culture, graceful, and numbers her friends by the score. Edith is equally popular and admirable, has hazel eyes, is a blond, tall and graceful. She is a gifted singer, talented, and is generally admired.

Miss Mamie Dierker is the daughter of George Dierker, a retired hotel keeper. She graduated in literary and music at the Synodical College, Fulton, Mo., and is a fine singer. She has wealthy family connections. She has dark hair and eyes, [is] graceful and a splendid entertainer.

Miss Gertrude Smith is the daughter of Capt. D.K. Smith, a merchant. She has dark hair and eyes, is a decided brunette, with lovely form and sweet manner, enviable musical talent, and enjoys a host of admiring friends. She has good family connections.

Miss Annie Hitch is the daughter of J.J. Hitch, but lives with her uncle, G.B. Hitch. She has dark hair, blue eyes, is a brunette. Enjoys prominent family connections, her uncle, G.B. Hitch, being a prominent landowner and stock raiser. She is graceful and a talented singer, very pretty, and one of the most popular ladies in the city.

Miss Claudia Harris is the only daughter of the late Dr. and Mrs. J.D. Harris. Her features are perfect and she has dark hair, brown eyes, a very fair complexion and is of medium height. She is a graduate in instrumental and vocal music of St. Louis and St. Charles, is organist at the M.E. Church and has a most excellent voice.

The Story Behind the Story

by Gerry Matlock

Recently, Octavia Evans Sigman of St. Louis, daughter of Dr. and Mrs. J.T. Evans, who resided in Wentzville from 1876 to 1901, donated many fine historical articles, souvenirs and pictures pertaining to Wentzville. One of the articles appeared in a 1934 edition of the *Wentzville Union*. This article referred to an issue of the *St. Louis Post Dispatch* published on December 12, 1895, nearly eighty years ago. My wife and I visited the St. Louis Public Library, and after searching through their microfilm files, there it was: "Society Belles of Wentzville, Mo." Nearly a half page was devoted to Wentzville society, with photos of five of the most prominent Wentzville belles.

Chapter 6

Men of Wentzville, 1855 to the Early 1900s

This chapter contains both articles that were written by Gerry Matlock during the 1960s, '70s and '80s and articles written within the last five years by Lois Kessler and Kathy Weindel. Many of Gerry Matlock's articles were published in the *Wentzville Union* and the *Messenger-Tribune*. Lois's and Kathy's articles were written for the Wentzville Community Historical Society's (WCHS) Cemetery Tours, the WCHS Facebook page or specifically for this book

The Cannons: Five Generations in Wentzville Area

By Gerry Matlock

Originally published in the Wentzville Union, *March 9, 1977*

Curtis Cannon, past president of the Wentzville State Bank, lived in this community most of his life. He looked with great pride upon the history that his parents, grandparents, great-grandparents and great-great-grandparents have played in our community.

The Cannon family was one of the first white families to settle in the middle eastern part of Missouri. Curtis Cannon's great-great-grandparents Joseph Cannon (1760–1843) and Nancy Sitton Cannon (1765–1845) were both born and married in North Carolina and first settled in Tennessee.

In 1811, the family moved on through Kentucky and the Mississippi basin. They continued to a point above the junction of the Missouri and Mississippi Rivers, crossing the Mississippi east of the present site of St. Charles.

Their first permanent home was built in 1811 on Big Creek, in what is now St. Charles County, about five miles north of Foristell. The first home was built by Curtis Cannon's great-great-grandfather Joseph Cannon. This is where three generations lived until their grandson George M. Cannon, grandfather of Curtis Cannon, built a home at the close of the Civil War in 1865. Curtis's father, James T. Cannon, was born in this first small cabin in 1865 just before the family moved to a new home. See page 24 for a picture of the first Cannon log cabin, built in 1811. The cabin no longer exists.

During the War of 1812, when Indians attacked the settlers, Joseph Cannon and his family lived in Kennedy's Fort, located in the vicinity of Wright City, where they remained until it was considered safe to return to their homestead. Joseph was a great hunter and Indian fighter and had many great adventures necessary for survival of a family in this wild country during this time.

One of Joseph's five children was Phillip S. Cannon, Curtis Cannon's great-grandfather. Phillip, born in Tennessee in 1809, was at a tender age when his family came to Missouri. After he grew up, he married Elizabeth

A 1902 Cannon family reunion at the home of George and Sarah Cannon, Moscow Mills. George and Sarah are seated in the center of the front row. Curtis, one year old, is held by his father, James, in the center of the back row. *WCHS Collection.*

McCoy, of another early pioneer family. She was born in 1812. They reared a family of ten children. Phillip was a farmer, an occupation in which he had substantial success. He left a comfortable estate at his death in 1856. Elizabeth died in 1849.

George M. Cannon, one of Phillip S.'s sons and Curtis Cannon's grandfather, was born on the old homestead in 1830 and built the second Cannon home in 1865. This home was a two-story house that was located on the Cook Farm north of Foristell. Reared on the farm, George thus acquired that taste for farm life which led to great success. While farming, he also had a specialty in raising stock. The old family homestead consisted of 310 acres, with 140 acres nearby and 230 acres in Pulaski County. In 1858, George married Miss Sarah Catherine Lewis, who was born in 1840, daughter of James and Elizabeth (Gross) Lewis of this county. The George M. Cannon family had ten children: John E., a practicing physician; Nance E.; Sarah E.; James T. (father of Curtis Cannon); George R.; Phillip S.; Oma May; Daniel W.; Albert B.; and Lucy A. George M. died in 1906 and his wife, Sarah, in 1921.

James T. Cannon, father of Curtis, the fourth child of George and Sarah, was born in 1865. He grew up on the farm and later bought a farm where Mid America Raceways is now located. (As of 2024, Mid America Raceways, located off Scotti Road, no longer exist. It is now a subdivision.) He married Frances Mae Wilkinson, and on January 17, 1901, a baby boy, Curtis Cannon was born. The family moved to Foristell around 1908. Curtis attended a business college in Iowa, returned to Foristell at sixteen years of age and began working in the Foristell Bank. During the first half of the 1900s, Foristell was a booming railroad town where farmers brought their crops in for shipment to the market. Besides the bank, there were three stores and two blacksmiths.

Curtis married Clara Borgelt in 1928. Her parents were Edward and Olinda (Schemmer) Borgelt, an early pioneer family of Cappeln. The Foristell Bank sold out in 1942. It was one of the few banks that stayed open throughout the Depression. Curtis joined the Wentzville State Bank in 1942 and became president of the bank.

The Cannon Farm was the family homestead continuously for three generations over a period of nearly ninety years. In the family cemetery on the old farm rest the grandparents, great-grandparents and great-great-grandparents of Curtis Cannon.

Over the years, the Cannon family has had three major family reunions. The first was in 1902 at the home of Mr. and Mrs. George M. Cannon in Moscow Mills. All their children and many great-grandchildren were present.

The second major reunion was held in 1938 at the home of James T. Cannon in Foristell. In the afternoon, all visited their old home place north of Foristell. A bountiful dinner of fried chicken, country ham, salads, pickles, etc., with cake, ice cream and peaches, was held.

The third reunion was held in 1973 in memory of their forefathers at the home of Mr. and Mrs. Curtis Cannon of Wentzville. Again, the home place and cemetery were visited. The evening was spent visiting with relatives, ending a happy day.

Henry William Karrenbrock, Immigrant Miller

Compiled by Gerry Matlock
Originally published in the Wentzville Union*, August 6, 1975*

Henry William Karrenbrock was born in the province of Westphalia, Germany, on June 19, 1829. As a youth of fifteen years, he immigrated to this country with his parents in 1844; they settled near Cappeln, Missouri.

He was married to Miss Clara Elizabeth Klaustermeier on September 23, 1853. This long and happy union was blessed with twelve children:

1. Catherine Mary (1854–1936), who married William Will (1856–1936);
2. Henry G. (1856–1947), who married Elsie Gerdemann (1858–1948);
3. Anna Wilhelmine Minnie (1858–1942), who married George Gerdemann (1851–1932);
4. Herman W. (1860–1939), who married Louise Knippenberg (1862–1928);
5. Caroline Louise Lena (1863–1944), who married Henry Riske (1859–1925);
6. Katherine Emma (1865–1945), who married John Weitkamp (1863–1946);
7. Augusta Louise (1867–1950), who married Henry Minor (1862–1942);
8. Elizabeth Christine (1870–1959), who married Henry John Buescher (1870–1958);
9. W.F. (Will) (1872–1952), who married Eugenia Harlow (1876–1970);
10. Charles Robert (1875–1964), who married Laura Ottie Hughes (1885–1969);
11. Martha Dorothy (1877–1959), who married Frank W. Hoener (1878–1956); and
12. Anna Olynda (1879–1967), who married John E. Frank (1881–1940).

Before reaching manhood, Henry William Karrenbrock developed a decided taste for mechanics. Following the natural bent of his mind and inclinations, he finally established in conjunction with his brother, G.W. Karrenbrock, who later lived at New Melle, a small mill known as a gristmill on the farm where they lived. It was a primitive affair, and after many tribulations and difficulties, Henry and his brother changed the location of the mill during the Civil War, securing a more accessible site on the St. Charles and Marthasville Road, about a mile below Gerdemann's store in Cappeln. Here they planned and erected, unaided, one of the best and most popular custom mills in the county. They built up and enjoyed patronage and, more importantly, a reputation for honesty and fair dealing.

Success and a bright future seemed assured until the introduction of the mill that was based on a "mill-roller system" changed the course of events. Henry and his faithful brother had to give way to the new inventions and progress. Almost past the prime of life, they were compelled to virtually start anew. They had to abandon the mill they had erected by their own hands and give up the very place that had been their happy home for so many years.

Undaunted, however, and mindful of their responsibility to their families and themselves, they set about to adapt to the new conditions. Both were eventually successful. G.W. Karrenbrock located at New Melle, Missouri around 1892 and in 1908, although well advanced in years, was still very active in business, enjoying good health and the well-earned fruits of fifty years of persistence and hard work.

Henry William located at Wentzville in 1892 and constructed and operated a roller mill here in the building presently occupied by the Acme Garment Company, located at the corner of Fourth and Elm. The building was a tobacco factory, first owned by Joel Carr. In 1894, the building became the Karrenbrock Milling Co., a flour mill. (See page 55 for the last image taken of the building before it was torn down. Only a marker remains.)

The Karrenbrock Mill built up a reputation that the family could feel proud of. Its leading brands of flour, White Cream and High Patent, were synonymous with quality, purity and honest weight and were favorites with many families in this section of the state. Age and failing health forced Henry to retire from the business in which he had been engaged for over a half century.

His two sons, Charles R. and W.F. (Will) Karrenbrock, assumed control of the mill. In 1907, Will sold his half interest in Karrenbrock Milling Co. to his brother, Charles. Charles, a practical miller and millwright, had been brought up in the business and continued to give his patrons the careful

Above: In 1894, this building became Karrenbrock Milling Co., a flour mill. H.W. Karrenbrock was noted for his honesty and fine products. *WCHS Collection.*

Right: Advertisement card for Karrenbrock Milling Company, which manufactured flour, meal and mill feed. *WCHS Collection.*

and considerate treatment that had been characteristic of the firm. Charles made several improvements at the plant by putting in new machines and remodeling and repairing others. Charles also built an elevator and warehouse by the railroad track on East Main Street.

Will went on to become a banker and president of the Wentzville Bank, which was located 6 West Main Street.

After an illness lasting several years, induced by complications of old age, which he bore with patience and true Christian fortitude, Henry W. Karrenbrock, surrounded by his beloved family, passed away peacefully at his home in Wentzville on November 13, 1908. He was seventy-nine years, four months and twenty-four days young. Services were held at the Wentzville M.E. Church, of which he was a devout member. He was known as a modest and unassuming man who practiced what he preached in his daily life and dealings with his fellow men.

Clara Elizabeth (Klaustermeier) Karrenbrock passed on November 6, 1915. They are buried in Linn Cemetery.

Ed S. Walker: Citizen, Banker, Friend and Counselor

By Gerry Matlock

Originally published in the Wentzville Union*, September 17, 1975*

Ed S. Walker was a lifelong resident of St. Charles County and a citizen of Wentzville from his boyhood days. He was not only a familiar figure on our streets and at the bank, but he was also looked upon as a most valuable friend and counselor by many of our residents.

Ed Walker is the son of Warren "Waddy" Washington Walker and Mary Milton Allen Walker. The Walker family is a very old pioneer family of this area. Ed Walker's paternal grandparents were Warren Walker and Mary Pollie Baker May Walker, early settlers of St. Charles County. His grandparents were from Rockingham County, North Carolina, and came to this county in 1831.

His grandfather was a successful farmer of the county and one of its highly respected citizens. His father, Warren, was born on the old family homestead in this county on July 4, 1838. He was brought up to the occupation of a farmer and in youth availed himself to the full benefit to be had in the occasional schools kept in the neighborhood. Having a marked natural taste for study and mental culture, he succeeded in acquiring more than an average education in the general English branches. Later, he became a schoolteacher. He had an excellent farm of about three hundred acres. They were members of the M.E. Church.

Ed's father was married in 1863 to Mary M. Allen, a daughter of Hon. William M. Allen, the founder of Wentzville. His parents had six children:

1. Warren Allen (1863–1942), who married Clementine Williams (1876–1966)
2. Ed S. (1865–1937), who married Helen Harlow (1874–1936)
3. Elizabeth Lizzie (1868–1940), who married Leland Lucey (1873–1939)
4. Cora L. (1869–1880)
5. Minnie (1870–1964), who married Harry R Towers (1875–1960)
6. Charles H (1872–1945), who married Laura S. Wise (1878–1975)

Ed was born on the Walker homestead on March 28, 1865. He was educated in the schools of St. Charles County and then attended Central College at Fayette, Missouri, and Bryant and Stratton Business College

Left: Ed Walker, pictured here in 1900, was a cashier at the Wentzville Bank. *WCHS Collection.*

Right: Genie Harlow (*left*) was one of the "Belles of Wentzville" and was married to W.F. Karrenbrock. Her sister Helen Harlow (*right*) was married to Ed Walker. *WCHS Collection.*

of St. Louis. After finishing his schooling, at the age of eighteen years, he accepted a position as clerk in the general store of Mr. Hudson, located on the southwest corner of Linn and South Main. The store, later owned by Ed's grandfather Warren Walker, was moved to the location of the Masonic building. Ed followed the mercantile business until 1905, when he and his brother-in-law, Will Karrenbrock, entered the banking business—the Wentzville Bank. He was vice president and director of the Wentzville State Bank at the time of his death on June 27, 1937.

He was married to Miss Helen M. Harlow, sister of Eugenia Harlow, one of the "Belles of Wentzville," at the M.E. Church South on November 8, 1893. Helen was born on April 7, 1874, in Mississippi. After the death of her parents, she was sent to Wentzville to live with her uncle Dr. J.T. Evans. The bride was considered one of Wentzville's most accomplished and lovable young ladies. Helen was a member of the Ladies Aid and always gave her best and spread sunshine and good cheer wherever she was found. She died on March 1, 1937. The Walkers are buried in Linn Cemetery.

John France

By Lois Kessler
Research by Mary Rowland and Lois Kessler

John France was born in St. Charles County, Missouri, around 1834. Not much is known about his life. It is thought he was born into slavery. The 1860 slave schedule suggests he may have been enslaved by William Frans. His mother, Ella, was born in Virginia. It is unknown who his father may have been.

The Civil War began on April 12, 1861. On January 1, 1863, Abraham Lincoln issued the Emancipation Proclamation. The proclamation announced the acceptance of Black men into the Union army and navy. In March 1863, two months after the Emancipation Proclamation, the government instituted a military draft and enrolled Black, as well as White, troops. In the winter of 1863–64, the Fourth Missouri Colored Infantry was organized at Benton Barracks, St. Louis, Missouri.

John France enlisted on March 9, 1864. The enlistment papers for the Colored Volunteers asked who each man had been enslaved by; when John enlisted, the word "free" was written in this space. His enlistment papers

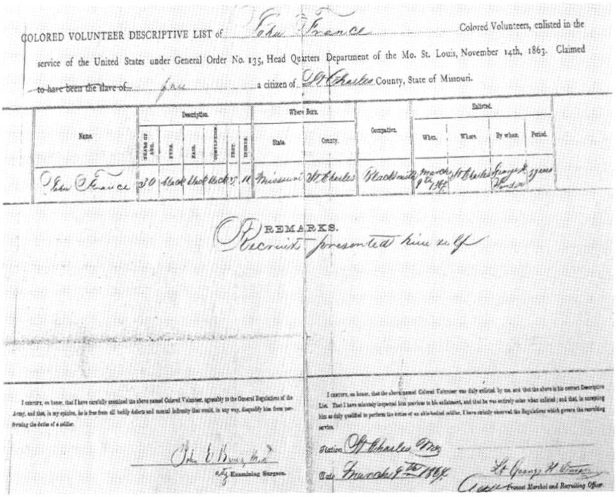

COLORED VOLUNTEER DESCRIPTIVE LIST of John France Colored Volunteers, enlisted in the service of the United States under General Order No. 135, Head Quarters Department of the Mo. St. Louis, November 14th, 1863. Claimed ~~to have been the slave of~~ free a citizen of St Charles County, State of Missouri.

Name	Years of age	Eyes	Hair	Complexion	Feet	Inches	State	County	Occupation	When	Where	By whom	Period
John France	30	black	black	black	5	11	Missouri	St Charles	Blacksmith	March 9th 1864	St Charles	[illegible]	3 years

REMARKS. Recruit presented himself

Top: "Colored Volunteer Descriptive List" of John France, who enlisted in the Colored Volunteers of the Union army during the Civil War. *National Archives, Washington, D.C.*

Bottom: Wood engraving of Camp Benton or Benton Barracks of St. Louis, established in 1861 and used throughout the Civil War. *Courtesy of Missouri Historical Society; Identifier P0084-0571.*

also indicate that he was five feet, eleven inches tall, thirty years old and a blacksmith. In the remarks section of his enlistment form, the recruiter wrote, "Recruit presented himself." His enlistment was for three years. He signed with an *X*. The 1870 census shows that he could not read or write.

John was a private in Company G, Sixty-Eighth Regiment. On April 27, 1864, the Sixty-Eighth was ordered to Memphis, Tennessee, and they defended the city until February 1865. There must have been a delay between when the orders were issued and when the troops left, because on May 20, 1864, John married Anna Pierce from St. Charles, Missouri, in St. Louis.

From July 5 to 21, 1864, some of the Sixty-Eighth troops were part of Smith's Expedition to Tupelo, Mississippi, to protect Sherman's supply lines for his Atlanta campaign. On July 14–15, 1864, the troops in Mississippi participated in the Battle of Tupelo and the Battle of Old Town Creek. It is unknown if John was part of the troops in Mississippi.

From April 1 to 9, the regiment was engaged in the siege and capture of Fort Blakely, Alabama. On April 12, 1865, they occupied Mobile, Alabama, after the surrender. At some point, the troops were moved to Camp Parapet, Louisiana. On February 5, 1866, John was mustered out from Camp Parapet. It is unknown what his muster out pay was, how he returned to Missouri or how long it took him to get back to Missouri and St. Charles County.

The 1870 census finds John and Anna living in the Flint Hill area with their nine-year-old son, William. This would indicate that William was born in 1861, possibly before it was legal for his parents to get married. The 1880 census shows John and Anna living in the Flint Hill/Wentzville area. John listed his occupation as farmer. Living with them were their son William, who was working as a blacksmith; John's mother, Ella; and three more children: Alice, Robert and Altona. The missing 1890 census is frustrating for researchers: it leaves a twenty-year gap from 1880 to 1900 from which family information is missing. However, the 1890 veterans schedules show that John was still living in the Flint Hill/Wentzville area and that in August 1890, he applied for a military pension as an invalid.

John passed away on March 31, 1898, in Wentzville. He is buried at Grant Chapel AME in Wentzville. He has a military marker, but it does not list day of birth or day of death.

In October 1898, Anna applied for a widow's pension. The 1900 census found Anna living with the George Wise family, working as a domestic servant. The 1900 census asked women how many children they had had and how many were living. Anna indicated that she had seven children and six were living. However, after the 1880 census, we could find no further references to any of the children mentioned in the 1880 census or the two or three additional children Anna would have had.

Goebel: A Legend in Photography

By Gerry Matlock
Originally published in the Wentzville Union
and the St. Charles County Record, *January 21, 1981*

Rudolph Goebel was a very well-known creative photographer who had his studio in St. Charles. He opened his studio in 1856 and retired in 1916.

He preserved over one hundred thousand negatives in his studio as he recorded the history of St. Charles County during his sixty years in the photography business. He lived in a time to see many of the towns in the county grow and witnessed many historic events.

Rudolph Goebel was a well-known photographer of St. Charles County from 1856 to 1916. *Courtesy of St. Charles County Historical Society.*

Goebel was born in Buer, Germany, in 1835. He received a public school education as well as four years of private instruction. He then went to sea and traveled around the world for four years. He arrived at New Orleans to clerk and then moved to St. Louis.

When he arrived in St. Louis, he met a daguerreotype photographer named A. Plitt. Goebel thought that at twenty years of age, he was too old to learn a new trade. Plitt, however, talked him into learning photography. Goebel left St. Louis in 1856, intending to travel around the country taking photographs. He arrived in St. Charles and decided to open his first studio.

He called himself a "portrait and landscape photographer." His first works were daguerreotypes (photographs produced on silver plates or silver-coated copper plates). Later, he made ambrotypes (pictures on glass) and pannotypes (pictures reproduced on patent leather). Later, he did tintypes and cartes de visite, small portraits three inches high that were used as visiting cards.

According to an article written by Edna McElhiney Olson dated February 22, 1962, published in the *St. Charles Journal*, "Goebel married his sweetheart Emily Dyers of Germany in 1859 and returned to St. Charles where he and Emily had eight children."

Goebel advised patrons how to get the best possible photographs: "Come in before you are worn out with the shopping or business. Dress in good taste and don't add too much. Bring your babies after a nap. Never come in late in the afternoon. Every face has its good points."

Nearby towns were too small to have a resident photographer; therefore, Goebel traveled throughout the county in his special wagon taking photos in these neighboring communities. In the early days, he used a light wagon that looked something like a U.S. mail car.

Above: The wagon that Rudolph Goebel used to travel to neighboring communities. Rudolph's employee would blow the horn to get everyone's attention. *Courtesy of St. Charles County Historical Society.*

Left: Picture of a Wentzville barbecue taken by Rudolph Goebel in 1886. *Courtesy of Missouri Historical Society; Identifier f5567.*

According to the Olson article, Goebel "opened a branch studio in Wentzville, Mo." The article does not state when the Wentzville studio began nor when it was closed, but Wentzville is fortunate to have had a Goebel studio at one time.

Goebel's Gallery stressed the number and variety of photographs available. He kept a large variety of albums, frames, cards, souvenir "postal cards," etc. He also carried many stereoscopic views, which were looked at through a stereoscope for a three-dimensional effect.

Around 1869, Goebel became the official photographer for the company building the Wabash Bridge across the Missouri River. He covered all major events in the community. For example, he covered the 1876 tornado, the opening and collapse of the St. Charles Bridge and the first car produced by the St. Charles Car Company, to name a few.

He was made a member of the Missouri Historical Society for his work. He was a member of the National Photographic Association and was praised as one of the very best photographers in the land.

Goebel was also one of thirty-seven liberal-minded citizens in St. Charles who put up $1,000 to help build a highway bridge across the Missouri River. He was an avid traveler throughout his life and spoke four languages fluently.

Mrs. Emily Goebel died in 1912. When Goebel retired in 1916, he sold his business to John Gossler, who had been his assistant since 1872. Goebel died in 1923 at the age of eighty-eight. All his children eventually left St. Charles.

Henry Michel, Forgotten Leader

By Lois Kessler
Originally published on the WCHS Facebook page, June 11, 2020

Henry Michel was a successful businessman in Wentzville for over fifty years. He was one of the leaders, a well-known, honest and well-liked businessman.

So who was Henry Michel? Born on April 28, 1842, in the Femme Osage area of St. Charles County, Missouri, he was the son of John and Mary Gruer Michel. His father was born in 1815 in Melle, Hanover, Germany, and immigrated to the United States in 1834 before coming to St. Charles County. John spent time in Baltimore, Maryland; Pittsburgh, Pennsylvania, and St. Louis, Missouri. He and Mary were married in 1841 and bought a tract of land near New Melle, Missouri, which they farmed until 1866. John and Mary had two children, Henry and Eliza Michel. John and Mary are buried in South Linn Cemetery in Wentzville.

Like most farm kids of his time, Henry went to school three or four months each year for about four years. When he was eighteen, he went to St. Louis and attended Jones Commercial College for two winters. After attending college, he clerked in a store in St. Louis for six months and then returned to New Melle, where he clerked for Henry Hensick for fifteen months. His sister Eliza was married to H.E. Dierker, who had a store in Wentzville, and when Henry left the employ of Mr. Hensick, he went to work for his brother-in-law. In 1868, he became partners with Dierker, and they renamed the store Dierker and Michel. They continued as partners

The big two-story building on the far right is Henry Michel's general store. *WCHS Collection.*

until 1872, when Henry sold his share to the Koenig brothers. He engaged in the grocery business in St. Louis and returned to Wentzville in 1876, where he purchased property on the corner of what is now West Main Street and Church Street.

In 1873, while in St. Louis, he married Matilda Brockman, whose father, Ernest Brockman, was a well-to-do farmer in the Wentzville/New Melle area. The Michels would have four children: Diena, born in 1874, who died when she was about six months old; Ella (1878–1953), who would marry Henry Wefel; John, who was born in 1879 and died in 1884 when he was not quite five years old; and Kate (1886–1978). Kate never married and lived with her parents until their deaths. While Ella was married, she and her family either always lived with her parents or in a house next to her parents that was owned by her father. The two other children are buried in South Linn Cemetery in Wentzville near their grandparents.

One of the first big fires documented in Wentzville occurred in 1882. At the time, a three-story building stood at the corner of what are now Pitman and Whitehead; Friendship Brewing Company now occupies this corner. The building housed the Methodist Church, the Masonic Lodge and the school. Henry had a lumberyard on the corner of Fourth Street and Church Street. A fire was discovered in the lumberyard. While the town was

Advertisement for the H. Michel Store, 1903. *WCHS Collection.*

distracted by this fire, a larger fire was started in the building on Pitman and Whitehead. The building burned, and the fire was suspected to be the work of an arsonist, who had started the fire at the lumberyard as a distraction.

Sometime between 1876 and the fire of 1882, Henry built the two-story building that stood on the corner of West Main and Church Street. A general store was downstairs, and the family lived in apartments on the second floor.

Today, almost 150 years later, a lumberyard still operates in this location. By 1906, Michel owned the land on the east side of Church Street from Main Street to Wagner Street and then east to Linn Avenue along Wagner Street. He also owned land on the west side of Church Street from Main Street to the Catholic church. The property on the east side held the Mercantile, his lumberyard, at least eight frame store buildings and property that he would later subdivide and plat as the Michel Addition. The property on the west side of Church held a furniture warehouse, several other warehouses and a two-story shop that was rented out by Mr. Michel and used as a saddle shop.

In 1883, a large tornado went through the Wentzville area, and many people lost everything. After the local citizens exhausted their resources to help the people devastated by this storm, a committee was formed to solicit funds from people in St. Louis; Henry Michel was on this committee.

In 1899, Henry Michel, J.H. Koenig and a Mr. Smith purchased six acres of land "west" of Wentzville for $1,630. This is the land where the second Lutheran church, the German Independent Evangelical Lutheran Church of Wentzville (now Immanuel Lutheran Church) was built. It fronts Pearce Boulevard and is now owned by the Wentzville School District. Henry Michel donated the bell that rang before every church service and when a member of the congregation died. While no longer used in Immanuel's new location, the bell has a prominent location on their grounds. In 1906, Main Street looked vastly different than it does today. In addition to businesses, many of which had living quarters on the upper levels, there were also single-family homes.

In 1906, a fire started in a barn behind the Henry Meyer saloon (Meyer Road is named for him). The barn was full of new-mown hay. It was believed that a worker who slept in the barn dropped a lighted cigarette. This fire almost wiped out the whole southwest side of Wentzville, which had no fire department or water system. It was fought by men with buckets of water. Calls went out to neighboring towns until almost three hundred men were fighting the fire. A call even went out to St. Louis asking for help from its fire department. At one point, according to newspaper reports, twenty-eight sticks of dynamite were used to blow up the furniture warehouse in hopes of stopping the fire. A fifteen-year-old boy fell off the second-story roof with no injuries. Seventy-year-old men were on the roof with him fighting the fire. Mrs. Dierker and Mrs. Wefel were under a doctor's care as they had been upstairs in the building when the fire started. People were carrying out things from the buildings, hoping to save what they could. The town was probably saved when the wind shifted. The Mercantile Store was saved, but it was estimated that property losses amounted to $32,000. Most of the lumberyard and Henry Michel's warehouses were gone. The value of his lumber alone was estimated at $14,500. Most of the loss was suffered by Henry Michel.

Maybe it was the fire of 1906 or maybe just age, but around 1910, Henry started divesting his business interests in Wentzville, and the Michel family, along with the Wefel family, relocated to Santa Ana, Orange County, California. Henry's sister Eliza had many Dierker in-laws who had also relocated from Wentzville to this part of California. Almost immediately, Henry started buying land.

In the early 1920s, the two families returned to Missouri, and they came to Wentzville frequently for business. Henry bought two houses next to each other in St. Charles, tore them down and built two new homes, one for the Michels and one for the Wefels. They'd been back in the area for only about a year when they returned to Southern California.

Henry Michel died on August 26, 1923, in Santa Anna, Orange County, California, and is buried at St. John's Lutheran Cemetery in Santa Ana, California. There is a Henry Michel buried in Washington, Missouri, and many people mistakenly think this is the Henry Michel from Wentzville, but that is incorrect. He left an estate of $37,000 (over half a million dollars in today's money). The estate consisted of new homes that had just been completed for his family and the Wefel family; other property in California and Missouri; stocks; and over $16,000 in cash. Matilda died in 1928 and is buried next to her husband.

George Kasper Henry William Dierker

By Kathy Weindel

George Dierker was born aboard ship while his parents, Victor and Clare, immigrants from Hanover, Germany, were crossing the Atlantic Ocean in 1842 on their way to the United States. Victor and Clare, with George and several siblings, arrived at the Port of New Orleans and then traveled up the Mississippi River and settled at Femme Osage, Missouri.

It was near Femme Osage that his father had purchased land to farm. George and his siblings spent their childhood growing up helping their father with the farm. Since their parents believed that their children should be able to read and write, George and his siblings were able to attend school together.

When George was sixteen, he and his older brother Henry moved to Wentzville. They had plans to become dry goods merchants, but things didn't go as they planned.

In 1861, the Civil War broke out, and George joined the Union army as a private in the Forty-Ninth Regiment of Missouri Union Volunteers, serving until the end of the war. When George mustered out, he had earned the rank of first lieutenant. During the last years of the war, George was serving in the army of the Gulf, whose purpose was to occupy the Confederate states that bordered the Gulf of Mexico. Some of his fellow officers took advantage of their positions, seized contraband Southern goods and sold them for a profit, which made them rich. George couldn't do such a thing, as his honor and respect were important to him, so he left the army poor in wealth but richer in honor.

When George returned to Wentzville in 1867, he built a wood frame hotel with the help of his family and began a career as an innkeeper. The name of the hotel was the Wentzville Hotel.

George knew the Peters family before the war and had the pleasure of seeing Henrietta Matilda Peters when she was visiting relatives in Wentzville after the war. Matilda Peters was born in St. Louis, Missouri, on October 15, 1849. Her parents were Franz Henry Rudolph and Catherine Elsebein Moentmann Peters, who had immigrated to the United States from Germany in the early 1840s. Her family lived in St. Louis, where her father was a feed merchant. Their family was active in the local Evangelical church, and Matilda attended its parochial school and then high school in the St. Louis public school system. Matilda first met George Dierker when she was seven years old while visiting her uncle Wilhelm and his family on their farm near Wentzville. Ten years later, when Matilda was seventeen, she saw George again. In June 1867, George and Matilda were married in her parents' St. Louis home. They returned to Wentzville, where they would build a life, a family and a hotel business.

Unfortunately, on New Year's Eve 1867, the hotel burned down. They never knew how it started; there were rumors that it was unattended lamp in the ladies' parlor or boys shooting off firecrackers.

Whatever the cause, it was a terrible loss, but George and Tillie decided to rebuild. They built a larger, three-story brick building with a hotel, saloon and restaurant. Not only would the hotel be their business, but it would also be their home for many years.

The hotel's location was excellent, near the railroad depot on the Wabash railroad line (North Missouri Railroad). It was located at the northwest corner of Linn and North Main (today Allen Street). Over the years, George and Tillie welcomed traveling salesmen, merchants and even the locals to enjoy their hotel, gather in the saloon and indulge in a fine Sunday dinner. The Wentzville Hotel was famous for its fine food (chicken dinners) and good hospitality. Working together, George and Tillie made it one of the most popular establishments in Wentzville.

Although George's main profession was that of a hotel owner, he was also involved in other organizations, businesses and politics. George, Tillie and their three daughters Clara, Eda and Mamie were active members of the Wentzville Methodist Church. George was a member of the Wentzville Masonic Lodge No. 46. George also served on the Dram Shop Liquor License Committee. He was a stockholder in the Wentzville Tobacco Company and served as its president in 1887 and one of its directors in 1888.

The hotel was used as a polling place, and George served as an election judge during the 1880s and 1890s. George was a member of the Democrat Party and, in 1886 and 1890, hosted the Democrat County Convention at his hotel.

Occasionally, something bad would happen that would upset the apple cart. One time, some of their guests were robbed of 1,200 cigars, clothing and money. George offered a reward of $100 for the capture of the robbers and the return of the stolen items.

The hotel was George and Tillie's home for over twenty years and where they raised their three daughters. George decided to give Tillie and his daughters a real home, so in 1897, he had a fine house built on Wall Street. They almost lost the new home during the 1915 cyclone.

Top: The Wentzville Hotel, pictured here in 1908, was owned and managed by George Dierker and his wife, Matilda. The hotel also had a saloon and a restaurant. *WCHS Collection.*

Bottom: The Wentzville Hotel's dining room, "a good place to eat." *WCHS Collection.*

When George and Tillie decided to retire, they hired Henry Salm to manage the hotel, saloon and restaurant. Eventually, George sold it all to William Heady. It would be called the Heady Hotel, and it remained a popular hotel for the city and its citizens. In the early 1970s, Heady Hotel was torn down.

On August 29, 1922, Tillie passed, and on January 12, 1927, George passed. A funeral service was held at his home, and then he was laid to rest next to his wife in South Linn Cemetery.

John Henry Koenig, Worthy Citizen of Wentzville

By Gerry Matlock and Lois Kessler

John Henry Koenig was born in Germany (Barkhausen, near Buer) in 1846. His father was H.F. Koenig Sr. and was born at the same location in 1820. H.F. Koenig Sr. married Mary Witkoetter, who was born near Melle, Germany. John Henry Koenig began business in 1873 in Wentzville and was blessed with a large measure of success. John was known for his high reputation for business honor and faithfulness to his word. During his early years in New York City (1865) and in Wentzville (1866–72), he also assisted his family members in moving to the United States.

Also living in Wentzville since 1842 were Clara Elizabeth Dierker (1799–1866) and Victor Dierker (1797–1865). It is not known if Clara was an older sister or paternal aunt to H.F. Koenig Sr., John Koenig's father. Clara Dierker, her husband and their seven children had traveled from Germany to the United States in 1842.

John Koenig was educated in Germany's excellent school system. In 1865, after the Civil War ended, he was determined to seek his fortune in America. He first went to New York City and obtained employment as a clerk in a grocery in Brooklyn. He remained there nine months and became well acquainted with the English language.

John came to Wentzville in 1866 and had little difficulty in obtaining a clerk position in the store of E.H. Dierker, located in the building today occupied by the IGA Food Locker on East Main Street at Elm Street. (As of this writing, the lot is occupied by the telephone company building.) He worked there for several years, earning a good reputation. In 1870, two of

John's younger brothers, Ernest Koenig and William Koenig, arrived in New York and traveled to Wentzville. His younger brother Ernest took John's job with H.E. Dierker in Wentzville, and John Henry then moved to St Charles City and worked there at another H.E. Dierker store for two more years. William Koenig started working at John Dierker's Livery near Wentzville and lived with Captain John F. Dierker.

In March 1871, John Henry applied for U.S. citizenship. In June 1871, another brother, Fred Koenig, arrived in New York and traveled to New Melle, where he lived by himself. Later records show that he married and raised a family in New Melle. Fred was a farmer.

In late 1871, John Henry returned to his home in Barkhausen, Germany, for nine months to help his parents and remaining siblings prepare for a voyage and move to Wentzville. In August 1872, the remaining Koenig family members arrived in New York. The family consisted of his father, H.F. Koenig, known as Fritz, fifty-one years old; his mother, Mary, fifty-two years old; his younger brother Hermann, fourteen years old; and his younger sister Lena, who was ten years old. Also traveling with the group was his oldest sister, Maria, who was twenty-eight, with her husband, Adam Wefel, who was thirty-three, and their two young children: Maria Wefel, three years, and Heinrich Wefel, four months. Also traveling with the Koenig family to the United States was Fritz Schmidt, sixteen years old. John's sister Lena and Fritz Schmidt would later marry and have six children.

After the entire Koenig family arrived in Wentzville, John and one of his younger brothers, Ernest, purchased Dierker and Michel Mercantile Store in Wentzville in 1872. Three years earlier, in 1869, H.E. Dierker had taken as a partner his brother-in-law Henry Michel. When John and Earnest purchased the store, they changed its name to J.H. Koenig and Brother Store. It was a general store that also sold furniture and lumber. The Koenig brothers ran the business together until 1893, when John bought out his brother Ernest's share. He went on to enlarge and improve the store's facilities.

In 1886, John built a home on land adjoining the store. It was a large, two-story brick home.

John's parents, Fritz and Mary, built a brick home in northern Wentzville and started dairy farming. This home became the family homestead. During the 1915 cyclone, Herman's son Harry K. Koenig and his wife, Martha Pfau, were living in the home. Martha Koenig was killed, and their family home was damaged. Martha is buried at the Koenig Cemetery in Wentzville.

This page, top: The Koenig home (*left*) and warehouse (*center*) and the J.H. Koenig Store (*right*). The store later became the Koenig-Buescher Store. (*right*) in Wentzville, 1907. *WCHS Collection.*

This page, bottom: Koenig-Buescher delivery truck in 1921. Employees are Jack Helldorfer (*far left*), Dave Edders (*driving*), Adolf Buescher (*on running board*) and Henry Schwede (*far right*). *WCHS Collection.*

Opposite, top: Herman F. (Fritz) Koenig and Mary Koenig's family homestead after they moved in 1872 to Wentzville from Germany. *WCHS Collection.*

Opposite, bottom: The Koenig family standing outside the parent's Koenig home on the north side of Wentzville. Herman F. (Fritz) and his wife, Mary, are the second and third from the left in the back row. *WCHS Collection.*

PORTION FARM OF HERMAN KOENIG
WENTZVILLE MO.

On June 17, 1873, John Henry Koenig married the widow Clara Elise "Lizzie" Dierker Schiller, daughter of John F. Dierker of St. Charles. Lizzie had married Frederick Matthias Schiller in 1870. Frederick died in January 1872. Lizzie and Frederick had no children. John and Lizzie were active members of the Lutheran church in Wentzville and had ten children:

1. Anna Marie (1874–1936), who married William Buescher
2. Dorothea "Dora" Karoline (1875–1953)
3. Lydia Marie (1877–1967)
4. Oscar Friedrich (1879–1915)
5. George Friedrich (1881–1936), who married Margaretha Heyn
6. Hilda Louise (1884–1884: nineteen days)
7. Ernest Victor (Hilda's twin, 1884–1884: seventeen days)
8. Gustave Wilhelm (1885–1920), who married Lillie C. Stoll
9. Albert Friedrich (1887–1968), who married Ella C. Hanson
10. Alfred Herman (1887–1887, two months)

Clara "Lizzie" died on December 10, 1890, leaving John with seven children ranging in age from sixteen to three. In January 1893, John Henry married Louisa Vossmeyer. Louisa was almost twenty years younger and had not been married before. John Henry Koenig and Louisa had three children:

1. Henry Friedrich (1893–1964), who married Clara Hilmes
2. Carl Wilhelm (1895–1968), who married Aurelia Vahrenhorst
3. Johann Erwin (1897–1981), who married Madolyn Hilmes

John died on April 13, 1897, five months before his youngest son was born. It was around this time that his brother William, who was married to Lizzie's sister Louisa, became the guardian to the three youngest boys, Gustav, Albert and Alfred. John and all three of his wives are buried at the Koenig Cemetery in Wentzville.

Ferdinand Goellner: Horse Trader, Stock Dealer

By Gerry Matlock
Originally published in the Wentzville Union, *November 26, 1975*
Further research added by Lois Kessler

Ferdinand "Ferd" Joseph Goellner was a successful businessman of Wentzville who dealt in horses and farm stock. The Goellner family, a well-known family of this area, is of Germany origin, and Anton, Ferd's father, settled near St. Paul on Dog Prairie in the 1850s. Anton's first wife died, and he later married Sophia Boos of St. Louis in 1863. Their union was blessed with seven sons and three daughters. The children were George, Anton Christopher, Ferd, William, Elizabeth, Frances, Henry C., Clemence, Joseph and Clarence.

Ferd Goellner was born in Dog Prairie on April 20, 1871. He worked on his father's farm, and that is where he first started trading in farm stock. Sometime before 1906, he came to Wentzville to help his brothers A.C. and William manage the Wentzville Hotel, later known as the Heady Hotel. In July 1906, Ferd traveled to Oklahoma and married his first wife, Leona McAtee. Like Ferd, Leona was raised in Dog Prairie, but she was living in Oklahoma when they got married. After the wedding, they returned to Wentzville. Leona died on August 29, 1931. She is buried in Dog Prairie with her mother. Ferd and Leona had no children. Her tombstone bears an incorrect death date. Ferd's second wife was Mary Elizabeth "Lizzie" Willerding, who was born in Gilmore and had lived in the area her whole life. They had no children, but they were always helping children around the neighborhood.

Fine clothes and elegant cars were Ferd's trademark. His car was a familiar sight on the roads of St. Charles County during the first half of this century.

His home was located on the north end of Wall Street at 716 Wall Street in Wentzville. The home was originally that of George Dierker, of hotel fame, and Ferd bought it from him. The cyclone of 1915 destroyed the beautiful brick home. Ferd rebuilt the home, again of brick but not quite so large. The home no longer stands, and the Baptist church is now on the property.

Ferd died on February 14, 1942, at his home. He had gone out to start his car to take his wife to church. Unable to start the car, he came inside, sat down in his chair, remarked to his wife how cold it was and then had a heart

Ferd Goellner in his car with his wife, Leona. Ferd was a horse trader and farm stock dealer. *Courtesy of St. Charles County Historical Society.*

attack and passed away. Although he is no longer with us today, his colorful past will long be remembered.

Lizzie passed away on December 26, 1943. Both Lizzie and Ferd are buried at St. Partick's Cemetery.

THOUGHTS OF YESTERYEAR: THE KOTHE AND MOELLERING FAMILIES

Compiled by Gerry Matlock
Originally published in the Wentzville Union, *February 11, 1976*

I read a very interesting article recently written by Grace Caroline Johanna Kothe (née Fogarty), who, with her husband, Joe, lives at 802 South Linn in Wentzville.

The article told how their ancestors, the Kothe and Moellering families, lived years ago. The message in the article is very appropriate today as we celebrate the two hundredth birthday of our nation. The article follows:

Those of us who belong to the Kothe-Moellering Families have ancestors who migrated to America from Germany in the mid-1800s. The Kothe Family settled one mile south of Wentzville along Highway Z on a hill just south and overlooking Peruque Creek. The home was built of logs about 1861 by Fred Kothe, a farmer, and still stands today.

The Moellering family also came from Germany but settled near the town of New Melle. Their home was a four-room log house located seven miles south of Wentzville and one mile west of Highway Z. The home was added on to in later years and still stands today.

These families cleared their land by using a hand ax and chopping down trees. These trees were then used to build a log cabin on the land. This cleared land was also used to plant their crops of wheat, corn, oats and barley to feed their livestock and to sell for money. They plowed their land with a man walking behind a plow pulled by a team of mules or work horses.

They fixed a special spot for the family garden and a fruit tree orchard. All fruits and vegetables in those days were grown from seeds planted in the spring of the year. The produce consisted of peas, beans, carrots, turnips, beets, lettuce, cabbage, radishes, onions, potatoes, watermelon, cantaloupe, and strawberries, to name a few. Popular fruit trees were cherry, peach, pear, apple, plum and damson. Wild berries such as blackberry, raspberry, gooseberry and wild strawberries were a delight.

In the summer months, vegetables, fruits and berries were eaten fresh. Surplus food was canned for the family to eat during the winter months. Fruit was made into delicious jams, jellies and preserves. Some were cooked and put into jars. Apple butter was made. Syrup was also made from sorghum.

Meat was butchered in the fall of the year for use both during the winter and summer. Pork sausage was smoked or fried down and placed into crocks. Hams were sugar cured and smoked.

There was no electricity in those days, no refrigerators, no running water in homes, no bathrooms or inside toilets. The bathroom was a washtub behind the wood stove. The toilet was called an outhouse and located outside the house.

At night the light to see by was that of the coal oil–burning lamps.

All food was cooked on top of a wood-burning range. Pies, cakes, bread, rolls, coffee cake and cookies (those old-fashioned ginger snaps) were baked in the oven of this wood stove. This wood-burning stove also heated the kitchen and all the hot water used in the home, including the bath and dishwashing water. The remaining rooms were heated by small wood-burning stoves or fireplaces. Most bedrooms had no heat.

Clothing was washed with water heated on the kitchen range. In the summer months, water was heated in an iron kettle over an open fire outdoors. Clothing was washed in a tub with a washboard with homemade soap by hand, wrung out by hand and hung inside at times during the winter but mostly outdoors. Soap was made from lye, water and fat, by the family.

Store-bought items included flour, sugar, salt, pepper, coffee and spices that were bought with eggs from the farm. Cream, milk, butter and eggs were produced on the farm.

Most clothing was made by mother.

Mattresses were made of cornstalks or hay. Your pillows and bed covers were made from goose feathers plucked from geese on the farm.

Water was caught in gutters when it rained. The gutters ran into a cistern or well. Water was drawn from the cistern with a bucket on a rope or pumped by hand with a hand pump, as needed. These cisterns or wells were also used to keep milk, butter and cream cool and fresh.

For transportation you either walked, rode a horse or if the family went along, you had a spring wagon pulled by a team of mules or horses. For entertainment there were square dancing, playing cards, big family dinners, hunting, fishing, swimming in creeks, ice skating and sledding parties.

Schools were one-room county schools for all eight grades. Very few children went as far as the eighth grade because they were needed on farms to work in fields or to help with the many chores around the farm home.

Mother did all chores in the home: gardened, washed, fed the chickens, ironed, cooked, baked, sewed, canned and made butter. She was helped by the children.

Father worked from sunup to sundown. He plowed the fields, planted the crops, harvested the crops, stored them in barns and corncribs, made silage in a silo for livestock and to sell. He raised cows, pigs and lambs for meat and to sell. He chopped all the wood used in the home; built fences, gates; repaired harnesses, wagons and the family shoes. He milked the cows. Naturally the children helped their father.

They rested on Sundays, went to churches of their choice, had big family Sunday dinners and visited their parents and grandparents, traveling eight and ten miles and back by horse and buggy.

They were good people. Yes, they had human faults, but you had respect and admiration for every one of them. They were hardworking, law-abiding citizens of the United States. They had respect for their church leaders and public officials.

Remember your ancestors in your prayers.

Milton Asberry Gannaway, Farmer/Stock Raiser

By Gerry Matlock and Lois Kessler

Milton's father was Francis R. Gannaway, a native of Virginia. Francis was seven years of age when he came with his father to Missouri. He lived until he was twenty years old in St. Louis County and then settled on a tract of land of which three acres had been cleared. Francis improved and continued to clear the land until it grew to become 320 acres. In 1850, Francis married Martha Ferney, likewise a native of Virginia and daughter of Milton Ferney, one of the first settlers of St. Charles County. Mrs. Martha Gannaway died in 1872, leaving three children: Milton A.; Edmund, a bookkeeper in Wentzville; and Francis R.J. Jr., a farmer in Oregon County, Missouri.

Milton A. Gannaway was born in 1851 near Femme Osage in St. Charles County. His early education was obtained at home. When seventeen years of age, he began his studies at the Wentzville Academy and continued there for three years.

On April 20, 1876, Milton Gannaway married Mary Imogene Talbott of Pauldingville, St. Charles County, at Orchard Mansion, which, according to the papers, was located about five miles south of Wentzville and was the home of her maternal grandfather, Preston McRoberts. The *St. Louis Globe-Democrat* reported on the wedding. According to the paper, Milton was "one of the most prominent and respected young men of St. Charles County."

Milton Gannaway feeding his chickens on his farm. *WCHS Collection.*

About Mary, who was called Genie by family and friends, the paper reported, "Among other good qualities is noted as being one of the most beautiful young ladies in Northeast Missouri." Sadly, Mary Genie died two years later, in 1878; she is buried in the Methodist Cemetery in Flint Hill, Missouri.

The Gannaway family were members of the Southern Methodist Episcopal Church, to which they were liberal contributors in work, interest and money.

In 1880, Milton moved to Wentzville. For a while, he taught school, and for six months, he engaged in selling machinery for J.C. Johnson of Wentzville. Next, he went out on the road as a salesman for the Carr and Dula Tobacco Co. of Wentzville. He continued this job for three years. Next, Milton conducted a livery business, buying out the establishment formerly owned by Purl Parker. He continued this venture for four years and then sold out, directing his complete attention to farming and stock raising.

Milton's second wife was Ella Wilson Ashbrook. She was the daughter of James Edward Ashbrook, a member of the firm L.L Ashbrook & Co., one of the oldest pork-packing companies in St. Louis, and Mary Tabitha Mathews. They married on July 30, 1884. Her mother would die a year later of a stroke at the Mathewses' home in Wentzville. Ella's maternal grandparents had bought a home and acreage from William Allen on the east side of Wentzville. Their property, which would come to be known as the Gannaway Farm, was located just south and west of the Southern Air Restaurant; it later operated as a satellite campus for Lindenwood College and will be torn down for the Mercy Hospital Complex in Wentzville. In 1895, Milton's farm was described as "finely improved and well adapted for general agriculture and the raising of livestock."

According to a niece of Ella's, she always addressed Milton as Mr. Gannaway but waited on him hand and foot, even laying out his clothing. When Ella passed, Milton struggled to do routine tasks that Ella had always done for him. Another of Ella's habits her niece remembered was that she would line the outhouse with pretty pictures from magazines and catalogs.

Ella Ashbrook's sister, Pearl, married Richard King II in 1883 at Wentzville. Richard was the son of Captain Richard King, who founded the famous million-acre King Ranch of Texas. After Ella and Pearl's grandmother Elizabeth Garey Mathews passed away, King purchased the property from the Mathews estate. The Gannaways lived there year-round, and the King family spent many of their summers at the Gannaway Farm.

The picture below is of Milton Gannaway and Richard King II visiting in the front yard of the house. The picture on the next page is of the King family on their front porch, but from far away, so that you can see the home.

Milton Gannaway outside of his home, which Richard King II purchased. This house was built by William Allen in 1855–56. *WCHS Collection.*

The family of Richard King II on the front porch of the Gannaway-King home, 1916. *WCHS Collection.*

The Kings and the Gannaways were a familiar sight in Wentzville between 1880 and the late 1920s. Ella died in 1928; Milton died in 1929. They are both buried at Bellefontaine Cemetery in St. Louis, Missouri, along with Ella's parents and grandparents and the Kings. They had no children, thus ending the history of the Milton Gannaway family of Wentzville.

Alex Hemmer: Hunter and Farmer

By Gerry Matlock
The Wentzville Union, *November 12, 1975*

The name of Hemmer is very well known in this community, and members of the Hemmer family were early pioneers of the Wentzville and Dardenne area. One of the subjects of this article is the third generation of Hemmer pioneers of this community: Alex Hemmer.

Part of the land now occupied by Lake Saint Louis was originally Spanish Land Grant No. 54, given to C. Zumwalt, according to the book *History of*

St. Charles, Warren, and Montgomery Counties, published in 1885. Much of this land was purchased by the Hemmer family during the 1800s and is known as the Hemmer Homestead.

Alex's great-grandfather was Herman Joseph Hemmer, and he was the first generation of Hemmers to migrate from Germany to the United States. He is also considered one of the first men to be buried in the Dardenne Church Cemetery, as his grave is located in the front northeast corner of the lot.

Alex's grandfather was Joseph H. Hemmer Sr., born in 1833, who married Fridiedaricha Schroer, who was born in 1839. She died in 1880. Joseph Hemmer Sr. then married Elizabeth Eisenbath, who was born in 1859. Joseph Sr. died in 1898, and his second wife died in 1927.

Joseph H. Sr. and Fridiedaricha had a son named Joseph Jr., born in 1858, who married Theresa Eisenbath in 1882. This union was blessed with eight children: Al, Fred, Bernadine, Leah, Alex, Emma Hemmer Bauer, Martha and one child who died as an infant. Joseph Jr. died in 1902, and Theresa died in 1928.

Alex, like his father and grandfather, was a great hunter and farmer. They lived off the land and were close to nature. Foxes and wolves were Alex's

The old Hemmer homestead in Lake St. Louis, 1882. Note the log walls of the house. Alex's grandmother Hemmer and mother, Theresa, are visiting. *WCHS Collection.*

favorite game, and he always owned four or five prized hunting dogs. St. Louisans would come for a chance to kill a fox or a wolf to take to the city and boast to their friends.

The hunting ground was the area south of Highway 70 where Lake Saint Louis is located. There were acres of woods, and the game was abundant in the old days. Alex is also remembered for finding and catching a bear on the grounds of Lake Saint Louis. A truckload of bears passed through this area in the early 1930s, and the driver stopped at the Old Trails Restaurant in St. Charles. While the truck was stopped, one bear escaped. About a week later, Alex Hemmer was checking on a sow and pigs in the woods on his farm when he came upon the bear attacking the sow. Alex had a coon dog with him, and the dog chased the bear up a big oak tree. Alex sent for eight to ten men from O'Fallon to bring big tarpaulins. When the men arrived, they spread the tarpaulins under the tree. One of the men got a big stick, climbed up into the tree and poked at the bear until he finally jumped. When the bear hit the ground, all the men threw the tarpaulins over him and jumped on him. They tied his feet and muzzled his mouth. They took the bear to the Hemmer Homestead and chained him to a post. The bear weighed about 125 pounds when caught.

Nobody claimed the bear, and Alex kept him for about two years. The bear grew to 225 pounds. People used to come for miles to see him. However, when the Hemmers were not home, people used to tease the bear, and he became quite mean. Alex figured it was time to get rid of him before the bear hurt someone.

A big wooden cage was made, and the bear was placed in the cage, which was tied to the running board of the Hemmers' car. It was a sight to see the car going to St. Louis with the cage and the bear tied to the running board. Hemmer sold the bear to the National Pet Shop on Olive Street near Grand Avenue in St. Louis for about one hundred dollars.

Alex met Hazle Cannon, and they were married in 1920 at the Dardenne Catholic Church, which his family had attended for many years. This union was blessed with five children: Gorene Hemmer Call, Clarence, Reginald, Helen Hemmer Schnyder and Irene Hemmer Heinlie.

According to Hazle, the early 1900s on the farm were filled with the fun of bringing in the harvest, enjoying the fine animals, making apple butter in copper kettles, hunting, eating holiday feasts and attending nearby weddings and church picnics. Alex and Hazle still lived at the Hemmer Homestead in the 1930s when weatherboards were placed over the logs and additions were added.

The Hemmer homestead in the 1930s. Weatherboards were placed over the logs, and additions were added. You can see the hitching post still standing. *WCHS Collection.*

Alex and Hazle moved out of the old Hemmer Homestead around 1958, and it was torn down in the early 1960s to make way for modern homes and apartments. Alex died on November 26, 1965. Hazle passed on February 26, 1979. Both are buried at St. Patrick's Cemetery in Wentzville.

Charles Edward Musick, a Farm in Town

By Gerry Matlock
Originally published in the Wentzville Union, *June 25, 1975*
Additional research and facts by Lois Kessler

Charles Edward Musick was born in 1858 in Fee Fee, St. Louis. In 1872, the Musick family moved to Dardenne. He attended St. Charles College in St. Charles, Missouri. Charles married Florence "Flora" Lee of Wentzville on April 26, 1882. She was born in Port Jervis, New York, in 1859 and came to Missouri in 1866 with her family, who settled in Wentzville. Her father was Philip Lee, who had a tailor shop here. For a year after their marriage, they lived and farmed in Dardenne.

In 1883, the Musicks established the family home on the west end of South Main Street. It was a "farm in town" within the corporate limits of the city. It was used partly as a dairy farm. Five children were raised there:

1. Alma (1883–1970), who married Charles Richards
2. Philip Lee Musick (1887–1974), who married Elizabeth Hasbrook
3. Alice (1889–1980), who married Verno Pitts
4. Floy (1891–1893)
5. Corinne (1897–1983), who married William A. McCracken

Charles was a busy man. In addition to running a dairy farm, he served as mayor of Wentzville (1904–05), an alderman and the town marshal. He was a member of the school board and an officer of the Methodist church. He also had a business in Wentzville called Chas. D. Musick's Livery Feed and Sale Stable. He operated the livery business until cars became the main means of transportation. Charles retired in 1919. Flora was known as a "loving, kind, and unselfish character willing to help anyone in need, especially the sick."

In 1923, the Musicks built a brick home at 506 South Linn Avenue. Later, they sold the farm to their son-in-law Charles Richards. During World War II, twenty-five acres of the ground was leased to the Farm and Home Administration to develop housing for workers at the TNT plant in the Weldon Spring area. This government housing project was called Oak Park. In 1957, the acreage that was Oak Park was sold to the Farm

Charles Musick had a livery barn/stable from 1907 to 1920 in Wentzville. The person on the left is unidentified; Charles is in the center and George Moellering is on the right. *WCHS Collection.*

and Home Administration. Later, another twenty-five acres was sold to the Wentzville Community Club.

On July 17, 1929, at about 3:55 p.m., while Charles was crossing the railroad tracks from the south side to the north side on the way to get his mail from the post office, which was in the Schierbaum building at the corner of Linn and Allen Street, he was struck by a westbound local freight train (no. 71, engine no. 242). The train had slowed in preparation for stopping at the train station, which in 1929 was located on West Main. It was speculated that due to his deafness, Charles had not heard the train. He had been crossing the railroad tracks at that location for over forty years.

After her father's death, Alma and her husband, Charles Richards, moved in with her mother at the house on South Linn. Flora passed on March 19, 1931. After Flora's death, the Richardses bought the home on South Linn. The Musicks are buried in Linn Cemetery in Wentzville.

A Pioneer Family: The Bueschers of Wentzville

By Gerry Matlock
Originally published in the Wentzville Union*, October 29, 1975*

Charles H. Buescher identified with the history of Wentzville as early as 1882. He was born in Holzhausen, Amtsbezirk Melle, Osnabrueck, Germany, and came to America on December 1, 1881. He lived with relatives at New Melle until February 16, 1882, when he came to Wentzville. Here he was employed in the mercantile store of J.H. Koenig and Bro. This business was on the block located on East Main Street between Elm Street and Whitehead Street. The telephone company now has a building located in this block. The mercantile store originally started under the firm name of Dierker and Peters (Ernst Dierker and Rudolph Peters). Later, Henry Michel bought Mr. Peters's interest, and when Mr. Dierker was forced to retire because of failing health, Henry Michel moved his stock into quarters where the Wentzville Mercantile operated at the southeast corner of Church and South Main. Then the firm of Koenig and Bro. was established.

Charles Buescher paid a visit to the fatherland in 1889. On the return journey, his ship was partially wrecked. Upon his return, he resumed his duties at the same store and, in 1897, bought an interest in the business, changing the name to Schemmer, Buescher and Co. On November 27,

The Buescher family. *Left to right*: Carl, Mary (Wefel), Elise (Lizzie), Adolph, Charles and Olga Buescher. *WCHS Collection.*

1890, he married Miss Mary Wefel, daughter of William Wefel, who lived on what was in 1934 known as the Pilgrim place south of town. She was also born in Germany.

Charles Buescher's union was blessed with four children: Adolph, Carl, Elise and Olga (Mrs. Henry Doepel).

Charles had five brothers, three who remained in Germany and two who came to the States. Mary had nine siblings:

1. Henry, who married Ella Louisa Michel (Henry Michel's daughter)
2. Johann (1873–1874)
3. Ernest, who married Susan Moellering
4. Emma, who married Henry Schwer and William Faber
5. Lena, who married Charles Stoll
6. William (1881–1882)
7. Lydia, who married Fred Kammeier
8. Ida, who married Alfred Meier
9. Dora, who married Harry McElhiney

In 1934, the *Wentzville Union* interviewed Charles for a historic chapter of its "Good Old Days" feature. Charles had vivid recollections of the past and was pleased to talk about the "old days." The following information is taken from that interview.

When Charles Buescher made his home in Wentzville 142 years ago,

> The community presented a different picture than we find today. Few of the "old landmarks" are still here today. The Heady Hotel building (torn down in the 1960s) was located on the now vacant corner lot next to the Sears store [West Allen Grill as of 2024]. George Dierker erected it and it was known as the Wentzville Hotel. Mr. George Freese supplied the first electricity to Wentzville in this building with a homemade generator. Schierbaum and Michael had a wagon makers shop. Henry Michel operated a general store in the Mercantile Store building on the southeast corner of S.W. Main and Church Streets. He also owned a lumberyard just south of the Mercantile building. The present Wentzville Lumber Co., operated for years by the Dickroegers, occupies the same location.

Charles Buescher continued in his 1934 interview:

> Justus, father of the late Fred Justus, operated a blacksmith shop on the lot just west of the present J and R Barber Shop. The Freese building used to be on this site but it burned down a few years ago. Fred Justus later moved his shop to the premises that in 1934 were the Jerome Parr Garage on S. Linn. William Oblerlag operated a saloon and Purnell Diggs operated a drugstore where the Heady butcher shop was located in 1934 (the Sears Store today). The drugstore burned down in the 1890s. Joel Carr and Robert Dula (father and son-in-law) operated a tobacco factory located just east of the (1934) residence of Judge John Brown. This factory was near the present Acme Garment Factory.
>
> Dr. Joseph C. Goodrich, dentist and grandfather of Goodrich and Preston Heady, owned a large frame building near Schierbaum's, later Rueter's blacksmith shop, part of which was used as a tobacco storeroom. This was destroyed by fire on December 10, 1892. The site of this building is the vacant lot just east of today's Marty's Fashions (the Schierbaum Building on East Allen and Linn). The Koenig-Buescher store received its name in 1914 when J.F. Koenig bought an interest in the firm.

> A large three-story building stood just south of the Koenig-Buescher store. The first floor was used for public school purposes, the second story was used as a Methodist church, and the third floor was used as a lodge hall by the Masonic bodies.

Charles Buescher recalled:

> On October 19, 1883, two raging fires in different parts of Wentzville threatened to wipe out the little town. It was at night on that date, when from unknown cause, the big lumberyard of Henry Michel was destroyed by fire. While the fire was raging and the citizens had gathered there, Mr. Buescher noticed a black cloud of smoke emanating from the Masonic quarters of the third floor just south of the Koenig-Buescher store. He was urged to run to the big fire and summoned help to save this building. Two great fires and no firefighting equipment; just buckets, axes, and a few ladders.

Charles Buescher ended his 1934 interview with the story of the fire:

> Robert Dula, the famous tobacco man, acted as fire chief and directed the work after the crowd had gathered. Every effort was made to save the building or at least the contents, however, little could be saved. Most of the Masonic records were destroyed. By covering roofs with blankets and pouring water over roofs of adjoining buildings they were saved. The combination church, school and lodge hall were completely consumed, as was the lumberyard. The tearing down of a high board fence next to the Koenig-Buescher store prevented that building from being destroyed. It looked like a "fire bug" had been at work. The wall of the Masonic building had been saturated with coal oil, and the supposition was that the lumberyard had been set afire to draw citizens away from the lodge hall.

Charles lived at 302 Whitehead and passed away on July 14, 1945, at the age of eighty-five. He was treasurer of the Immanuel Lutheran Church for fifty years.

One of Charles and Mary's children, Adolph E. Buescher, was born in Wentzville on September 10, 1893. He married Eugenie K. Stroh of St.

Charles Buescher, eighty-two years old, working in his yard, 1944. *WCHS Collection.*

Louis on June 10, 1920. She was born on June 5, 1894. Adolph and Eugenie lived in Wentzville at 102 East Koenig. He worked at the Koenig-Buescher store from 1911 to 1948, a span of thirty-seven years.

Adolph and Eugenie have both been greatly involved in community affairs. Adolph was an alderman for several terms and Wentzville Legion Post 323 commander from 1942 through 1944. Both are charter members of the Wentzville Community Club, which was formed in 1933. She is a past president of the Wentzville Business and Professional Women's Club, past president of the Lutheran Women's Missionary League–St. Charles Zone and past treasurer of the Immanuel Lutheran Church Ladies Aid. On December 8, 1969, Eugenie was elected the first woman president of the Wentzville Community Club and was president for four years. She also served as clerk for the City of Wentzville for seventeen years. Adolph and

Left: Adolph Buescher in his United States Army Air Corps uniform at the end of World War I, 1918. *WCHS Collection*.

Right: Adolph Buescher and his wife dressed in costume for the Homecoming Parade. *WCHS Collection*.

Eugenie are both members of the Lutheran church, and she has been an organist for forty years. Their marriage was blessed with three sons: Adolph Jr., Eugene and Robert.

The writer has known Adolph and Eugenie Buescher for more than thirty years and, as a child, lived in a section of the Buescher home. They have always spoken of the positive side of life, and I can never remember them saying a discouraging word about another person. They have always practiced the "Golden Rule" and have been very instrumental in the growth and progress of Wentzville. They may truly say that they did their share to promote the welfare of the town.

The Bueschers of Wentzville will always be recorded in our history books as very important pioneers of our community.

William "Bill" Rueter, Blacksmith

By Gerry Matlock
Originally published in the Wentzville Union, *May 28, 1975*
Additional research and facts by Lois Kessler

One of the second-generation (twentieth-century) pioneers of Wentzville was Bill Rueter. Bill was born on December 13, 1897, at Cooper Hill, Missouri. His father, Gustaf Rueter of Lippe Detmold, Germany, was born in 1861, and after serving in the German military, he migrated to America in the late nineteenth century. He settled in Cooper Hill and became a blacksmith. Here, he met and married Elizabeth Schneider, and they had eight children: Martha, Dora, Lena, Fred, Bill, Gus, Lydia and Harry.

Bill grew up in Cooper Hill and learned the trade of blacksmith. In 1918, he came to Wentzville. He immediately went to work for Ed Schierbaum, who owned the blacksmith shop, the hardware store and the building that housed the post office, of which Bill Meyer was postmaster. This block of land is located just north of the railroad tracks. Today, only the post office building stands, still called the Schierbaum building by the longtime residents of Wentzville.

Bill Rueter as a young boy (*front row, center*) with his siblings and family. *WCHS Collection.*

Portrait of Bill Rueter as a young man. *WCHS Collection.*

Bill recalled that in 1918, transportation was mostly by horse and buggy. Automobiles were still not abundant. The town had one Ford dealership, operated by Mr. George Freese of Wentzville. Horses were of two main types: those for riding and workhorses, which accounted for the majority. Tractors were also not abundant at this time.

In 1920, Bill married Erna Schlueter, born on February 9, 1900, of New Melle. She was the daughter of August and Christine Schlueter. August worked at the Karrenbrock Mill in New Melle. Bill and his new wife moved to St. Louis for a brief time, where he worked for the Sligo Iron Company. They came back to Wentzville in 1925, and Bill purchased the blacksmith equipment from Ed Schierbaum and leased the building. He renamed the shop W.C. Rueter, Blacksmith.

Left to right: Erna Rueter, Bill Rueter, and their daughter Elaine Rueter, in her World War II marine uniform (*center*) . *WCHS Collection.*

During the 1920s and '30s, the blacksmith shop was a remarkably busy place. For example, Bill recalled that in one day, he installed as many as forty-five new shoes on horses. I was amazed at the prices of those days. The cost of four new horseshoes, installed, was two dollars. Plow sharpening was twenty-five to thirty cents each. The cost of resetting wagon wheel rims was four dollars per wagon.

Bill and his wife also remembered the dances held in the hall located above the hardware store in the 1920s and '30s. Two of the band members they recalled were Vince Schroeder, who played the guitar, and Charlie Nunley on the banjo.

Bill was one of the early members of the Wentzville volunteer fire department, organized around 1928. From 1933 through 1935, he worked with other fine citizens of Wentzville in organizing our Wentzville Community Club, which was officially organized and began the annual three-day homecoming tradition in 1935. He was made a charter member of the club in 1935.

The blacksmith building was sold around 1940, and Bill moved his equipment to Oscar Schierbaum's building on Linn Avenue (which later became an appliance store and has since been torn down). It is said that this building was formerly a broom factory.

During World War II, the blacksmith business was sold to Carl Kammeier, and then Bill worked for the TNT, a gunpowder plant located at Weldon Spring, Missouri. He was employed by the plant during its initial construction and later as a fireman.

In the 1950s, he worked for the Phillips Oil Company of Wentzville and the West Side Refrigeration Company in St. Louis. Bill retired in 1963.

Bill and Erna Rueter had two daughters, Elaine Rueter Miller Swantner and Jeanette Rueter Reese; four grandchildren; and two great-grandchildren.

Erna also played an active role in the community. She took an active part in the Wentzville Community Club and worked at the public school cafeteria from 1950 until her retirement. In 1971, she helped organize the Meals on Wheels program in Wentzville, the first to operate in St. Charles County. In 1974, Meals on Wheels expanded to the Wentzville Christian Church building, formerly the Green Lantern Restaurant off Highway Z. In 1975, she was still active in promoting the welfare of elder citizens. Erna had several interesting hobbies to keep her busy. Her motto was, "Never throw anything away before you try to make something out of it."

Bill passed away on November 23, 1978. Erna passed away on February 18, 1988. Both are buried in South Linn Cemetery.

A.I. Schulz or Arthur Irwin Schulz Sr.

By Lois Kessler

Originally published on the WCHS Facebook page, December 17, 2016

Starting in November 1914, a series of ads appeared in the *Wentzville Union*. A.I. Schulz placed the ads. The first ad simply told readers to "watch this space" and ran on November 6, 1914. The second ad was a reprint of a letter informing Mr. Schulz that the "Special Tax Law" does not apply to straight whiskey. The final ad encouraged readers to place their orders for their "High-Grade Christmas Whiskey NOW good for Eggnog and Tom & Jerry's."

According to a talk Julia Ruebling gave to the St. Charles County Historical Society in the 1970s, the Wentzville Distillery was located south of the city limits across Perque Creek. The whiskey was corn whiskey made with fermented corn mash. Mr. Schulz also made soda water. The historical society has several whiskey and soda bottles on display.

So who was A.I. Schulz? Arthur Irwin Schulz Sr. was born in Centralia, Boone County, Missouri, on October 7, 1868. His father, C. Henry Schulz, was born in New Melle, and after spending some time in Centralia, the family moved back to the Wentzville/New Melle area. Sometime before 1900, Arthur married Louise Moritz. Louise was born in New Melle on February 15, 1872. Arthur and Louise would have four children: Sarah Frances, Arthur Jr., Bertha and Leona. Sadly, Sarah, who was born in October 1902, died in June 1906. Their son Arthur Jr. was born on January 12, 1912, and only lived eighteen days. Sarah and Arthur Jr. are buried in South Linn Cemetery. Leona married Arthur Sprank, and Bertha married Elmer William Minor. Elmer's mother was a Karrenbrock, and through the 1940s, he and Bertha lived on Linn Avenue. Early in their marriage, he worked at the bank (his uncle William Karrenbrock was president of Wentzville Bank); later, he worked for National Petroleum.

The 1910 federal census shows that the family was living on the Wentzville/New Melle Road; this would be Highway Z. Apparently the census taker did the census of the citizens of New Melle and then started coming up Z toward Wentzville. Arthur gave his occupation as manager of a distillery.

In 1920, prohibition was the law of the land, and in the 1920 census, the family is shown as living in Ward 2 in Wentzville; Arthur listed his occupation as real estate agent. There has been some speculation that the family home during this time was the brick two-story home that sits on the corner of West Allen and Church Street. I am not sure that this was their home. Their home may have sat across Church Street, where there was a wooden two-story house that has been replaced by a metal building. The 1930 census shows the family still living in Ward 2 in Wentzville; Arthur listed his occupation as operator of a filling station.

Arthur was the uncle by marriage of Melvin Moritz, and when Melvin was looking into starting his career, his uncle suggested he should get into petroleum, as cars were replacing horses as a mode of transportation. Melvin followed his uncle's advice, and Arthur also got into the business.

Arthur Schulz Sr. died on June 23, 1938, and is buried in South Linn Cemetery. His obituary states he was operating a gas station on U.S. 40 in Wentzville.

Above: Two men "testing" Schulz Whiskey. Date unknown. *WCHS Collection.*

Left: Empty bottles of Schulz soda. *WCHS Collection.*

Business card of A.I. Schulz. *WCHS Collection.*

The 1940 census shows Louise living in Wentzville on Allen Street and renting a room to a young man. At the time of her death on August 1, 1959, she was living with her daughter Bertha Minor. Bertha and her family were living in Springfield, Missouri. Louise is buried in South Linn Cemetery with her husband and her two young children who proceeded her in death.

William F. Karrenbrock, Wentzville Banker

By Gerry Matlock
Originally published in the Wentzville Union, *September 10, 1975*
Further research added by Lois Kessler

W.F. (Will) Karrenbrock was a well-known citizen and president of the Wentzville Bank and, later, the Wentzville State Bank. He was the son of Henry William and Clara Elizabeth Karrenbrock and was born at New Melle on November 17, 1872.

Top: William F. Karrenbrock and Genie Harlow Karrenbrock, one of the "Belles of Wentzville." *WCHS Collection.*

Bottom: W.F. Karrenbrock (*left*), president of the Wentzville Bank, and Ed Walker (*right*), cashier, standing at the cashier window of the Wentzville Bank. *WCHS Collection.*

Will and his brother Charles assumed control of the mill because of their father's failing health. Will sold his half interest in the Karrenbrock Milling Co. to his brother around 1905. On November 12, 1902, Will and Miss Eugenia Harlow, one of the 1895 "belles of Wentzville," "stole a march" on their friends by leaving on the early train for St. Charles, where they were married. After an elegant supper at the home of Mr. Ed S. Walker, brother-

The Wentzville Bank, pictured here circa 1917, was originally at East South Main. *WCHS Collection.*

in-law of Will and his wife, the former Helen Harlow, they went directly to their lovely cottage on South Third Street.

Eugenia was born in Mississippi in 1877. Her mother died in 1880, and for a couple of years, she lived, along with her sister and father, with her maternal grandparents in Mississippi. Her father remarried in 1883, but he died in 1886. Shortly after his death, Eugenia and her sister Helen were sent to live with their uncle Dr. James T. Evans in Wentzville. Eugenia also lived for a time with her uncle Eugene E. Evans in Mercedes, Texas. But after her sister married Ed Walker in 1893, she returned to Wentzville and lived with Helen and Ed until her marriage in 1902.

Early in life, Will became a member of the Methodist Church and served on the official board of the local church for many years.

In 1905, he and his brother-in-law, Ed. S. Walker, entered the banking business—the Wentzville Bank. W.F. (Will) Karrenbrock was president, T.A. Foster vice president and Ed. S. Walker cashier. These gentlemen, together with L.N. Marsh and Charles R. Karrenbrock, constituted the board of directors. Total liabilities were $52,460.35.

Will Karrenbrock died on July 5, 1952, at eighty years of age. Eugenia lived to be ninety-three; she died on May 17, 1970. The Karrenbrocks are buried in Linn Cemetery.

Alonzo Draine and Sister Ella Draine

By Lois Kessler
Originally published on the WCHS Facebook page, February 27, 2018

Alonzo William Draine (at times also spelled Drain) was a teacher at the Lincoln School in Wentzville. Alonzo was born in Montgomery County, Missouri, on May 5, 1874. While he was still a young boy, his family moved to Keokuk, Iowa. The family consisted of Alonzo; his parents, John and Mary Parks Draine; and his two sisters, Ella and Margaret (Maggie).

One report I read said that John was born in slavery in Clay County, Missouri, and that he escaped when he was eighteen and joined the Union army, fighting in several battles. I also read reports that in 1940, he was honored for being the last Black Union soldier in Keokuk.

In 1894, Alonzo graduated high school, and not long after, he started teaching at the Lincoln School in Wentzville. He also served as principal. He was in Wentzville for three years. He left in 1897, when he accepted a position with McGrath Brothers, a "drug house," which I take to mean a drugstore or pharmacy.

In 1900, Alonzo went to pharmacy school. He would graduate in 1902. Meanwhile, his sister Ella was teaching at Lincoln School in Wentzville. She also served as principal of the school along with teaching. She would later teach in St. Charles, St. Louis County and Jefferson City. Their younger sister Margaret died in 1913, but before her death, she taught in St. Louis County.

On April 14, 1903, Alonzo married Susan Rowan in Cape Girardeau, Missouri. They would have five children, four boys and a daughter. Sadly, three of their children died early. Their daughter Mary died at the age of four in 1911 of whooping cough. In February 1920, their one-and-a-half-year-old son, Bruce William, died of pneumonia. In December the same year, their seven-year-old son, Mathan Parks, died of influenza. Two sons, Elliot and Milford, survived and would live in St. Louis.

In 1907, Alonzo and his sister Ella had an ice cream parlor and drugstore in Keokuk, which they sold in 1911. In 1913, Alonzo took and passed the exam for mail service, and I found a reference to him working as a "special mail carrier" in 1915.

Over the years, Alonzo was active in his community: he served on the board of Bethel AME Church, was a charter member of the NAACP group in Keokuk and was active in the Masons and other organizations.

The last reference I've found to Alonzo Draine was in 1940, when he visited his sons Elliot and Milford in St. Louis, where they sold insurance.

CHARLES RICHARDS, "MR. WENTZVILLE," AND HIS WIFE, ALMA LEE MUSICK

By Gerry Matlock
Originally published in the Wentzville Union, *June 25, 1975*

A name prominent in the history of Wentzville is that of Charles Richards. His contribution to civic affairs here earned him the title "Mr. Wentzville."

Born on March 22, 1878, on the family farm several miles north of Wentzville, the son of Charles Thomas and Sarah Francis "Fanny" Givens Richards, he was educated at rural schools and at Buchanan College in Troy. His siblings were Gould, Dina (Justis) and Roma (Cannon).

In 1903, he purchased the *Wentzville Union* from W.H. Dickey, and the next year he was joined in ownership of the newspaper by Miss Lizzie Walker. Mr. Richards was editor of the paper until he sold out in 1910 to William Rohrkaste to become a salesman for the Graham Paper Company in St. Louis.

On October 1, 1908, Charles married Alma Lee Musick. They were married at the Shaw Avenue Methodist Church in St. Louis. Two years later, they moved to Waterloo, Iowa, where he continued his employment with the Graham Paper Company.

Returning to Wentzville in 1916, Charles built the brick house at 201 East Maple where he and Alma lived until 1929, when they moved into the Musick Home at 503 South Linn with her mother. They purchased the home in 1935.

In 1918, on his draft registration form, Charles listed his occupation as printer. He described his build as tall and slender, with brown hair and grey eyes. After working as a salesman for the Royal Typewriter Company, Charles founded the Missouri Typewriter Exchange in 1920, which he operated until selling the business in 1945 to F.D. Hagan. He continued to work as a salesman for the firm until his retirement in 1960.

Opposite: Alma and Charles Richards' wedding picture, 1908. *WCHS Collection.*

Above: Charles Richards' home on Linn Street, July 1935. *WCHS Collection.*

Right: Charles Richards in 1933. That year, he was the president of Wentzville's Community Club and was very busy fundraising and helping the community. *WCHS Collection.*

In the early 1930s, Charles became the first president of the Wentzville Community Club, a post in which he served for about ten years. During this time, he also was president of the Wentzville Lions Club. Long a promoter of the annual Wentzville Homecoming, Charles continued active membership in the Community Club and was reelected to serve another term as its president in December 1957.

Charles was chairman of the St. Charles County U.S. Savings Bond program for twenty years, a position he gave up at the end of 1961. For many years, he oversaw the Red Cross Bloodmobile program in Wentzville.

Charles and Alma were members of the Wentzville Methodist Church.

Death claimed Charles on April 23, 1963, and Alma on September 1, 1970. Both are "At Rest" in Linn Cemetery, in the Musick family lot.

The Heady Family of Wentzville

By Lois Kessler
Originally published on the WCHS Facebook page

Gideon Preston, or Pres, as he was known to friends, was born north of Flint Hill on July 12, 1895. Pres would say that prior to moving to Wentzville, his family were Mississippi River bottom farmers. The Heady family moved to Wentzville in 1912 when Pres was sixteen. The family consisted of parents William S. Heady Jr. and Nancy "Nannie" Goodrich and their children: Joseph Goodrich (Joseph always went by the name Goodrich); Mary; Roberta; Gideon Preston (who always went by Pres) and Nancy B. You could say that Pres was old-time Wentzville, even though his first sixteen years were spent north of Flint Hill. His grandfather was Dr. Joseph Carter Goodrich. His mother's stepsister (they never referred to each other as "step") was Julia Womack, who married Caleb Dula of tobacco fame.

Pres's father, William, was a busy man in 1913. He bought the hotel that stood on the northwest corner of Linn Avenue and Allen Street from John and Lou Willerding. In addition to the hotel, he had a commercial dairy business with a first-rate dairy barn, registered Jersey cows and the first electric milking machine in the Wentzville area, which was powered by gas (his sons worked the dairy). William had a registered bull he offered for stud service, sold horses, helped start a commercial club, was a foxhunter and raised foxhounds. Also, at various times, William was sheriff, deputy sheriff

The Cocktail Bar and Grill at the Heady Hotel. *WCHS Collection*

and game warden, sometimes acting as all three at once. In 1916, William bought the barn behind the hotel from Willerding and Bryan that was used for their livery business, installed a water trough and let people coming to town to shop or stay at the hotel use the barn for free. Willerding and Bryan moved their livery business.

In 1916, William built a building on North Main (West Allen today). The building was twenty-four by seventy-four feet, with a modern glass front and twenty-six electric lights. In May 1917, he held a grand ball there, and in May, he opened the building with a confectionery, restaurant and butcher shop called the Red, White and Blue Meat Market, Confectionery and Restaurant. William sold the dairy, and his sons ran the meat market and the other business in the building. The building still stands and today is Goat Pub on West Allen. William converted the dairy barn, which had a concrete floor, into a slaughterhouse where they butchered the meat they were raising (cattle, pigs, sheep, chickens, etc.).

While Preston and Goodrich always worked for their father, they often also worked at other establishments. For example, when he was young, Preston worked at the Mercantile Store.

The year 1917 was a busy one for Pres. In addition to running his father's new business with his brother, Pres had multiple things in which he was involved. He was secretary of the Wentzville Dance Club, going to dances dating Alma Rothermich and hunting with his friend Mike Bryan, who would become the chauffeur for the King family in Texas. He also registered for the World War I draft. To add insult to injury, he fell and broke his nose while chasing a chicken.

A young Preston Heady. *WCHS Collection.*

Pres was drafted in September 1918 and sent to Camp McArthur in Waco, Texas. His time in the military was short: he received his discharge in December 1918. As a veteran, he and others in Wentzville who served in World War I started the American Legion in Wentzville in 1920. At the time, the American Legion was a new organization. Pres was the first commander of Post 323 in Wentzville. In 1919, Pres, his brother and his father bought a new Ford truck, added a refrigeration unit and used it to deliver their meat.

In 1920, William, Pres's father, had a new frame building built between the hotel and the Red, White and Blue Meat Market, Confectionery and Restaurant. This building would later house John Duello's harness shop, and in 1945, John bought the building from the Heady brothers. John tore the building down and built a two-story brick building in its place. The building is now home to West Allen Grill. The Headys also built a forty-by-sixty-foot dance platform behind the Red, White and Blue Meat Market and the hotel and started holding dances. Pres began raising and selling bird dogs. Hunting, fishing and dogs were always important to him.

In November 1925, Alma and Pres finally married, and they honeymooned in Decatur, Illinois. Alma was thirty-three, and Pres was thirty. There may been impediments to this marriage: Alma was a staunch Catholic, and Pres was not. Alma was a Democrat and highly active in the Democrat Party. Pres was Republican and active in his party.

In 1926, William, while marshal, raided a still southeast of Wentzville and destroyed the still and gallons of mash. In July, William died of blood poisoning; he was sixty-seven.

William's death forced Goodrich and Pres, who were the executors of their father's estate, to sell some assets. They sold property on the courthouse steps, including the hotel. George Zollmann bought the hotel for $8,500.

The brothers were soon able to buy the hotel back and put their sister Mary and her husband, Zack Woods, in charge.

For most of their married life, Alma and Pres lived in an apartment in the hotel. But also, at various times, they had homes, mostly located on Allen Street. Pres's brother Goodrich, a lifelong bachelor, lived with them. They would never have children but were incredibly involved in the lives of their nieces and nephews.

Pres accidently shot himself in the leg in 1931 while coon hunting with friends. He climbed a tree to shoot a treed coon, and he put the gun in his pocket while descending. The gun went off and shot him in the leg. He was admitted to the VA Hospital in Jefferson Barracks, and he had surgery on the leg.

Following in his father's footsteps, Pres was elected marshal in 1932. He served as marshal from 1932 to 1936. During his time as marshal, he had bloodhounds that he used for the city, county and state.

Pres was instrumental in forming the Wentzville Volunteer Fire Department in 1933. The next year, the city appointed Pres fire chief. The year 1933 is also the year the Wentzville Community Club (WCC) was formed, and Pres was a founding member. In 1935, as part of the WCC, he was on the committee that started the first Boy Scout troop in Wentzville. In 1936, he was elected constable for Cuivre Township.

While Pres and Goodrich were busy with their business and Pres with various organizations, Alma was also busy. In addition to being a member of and holding offices in various Catholic organizations, the Democratic Chairwomen, bridge clubs and women's organizations, she was also very active in the WCC. Plus, there does not seem to have been a wedding, birth celebration, graduation, recital, convention or funeral that she did not attend.

By 1936, Pres and Goodrich had divested themselves of many of their businesses. They sold the meat market, which had moved one door east of the Red, White and Blue, to Edmund Dickherber. They also sold the Red, White and Blue building to Harry Thiemann (who had been operating a bar in the building since 1934).

In 1936, Goodrich went to work for Schramm's selling Chevrolets, and Pres went to work for Jim Weir in his radio and general repair shop. Pres ended up suing Weir for commissions due and won. In 1937, Pres opened a used car lot, calling the business Heady Sales and Service. By 1938, Pres was in business with Bob Swantner at Swantner Heady Implement Company. They sold equipment by McCormick-Deering and International Farmall.

Elected mayor of Wentzville in 1938, Pres served until 1948. When Pres was mayor, the mayor and the aldermen received twenty-four dollars a year. During his years as mayor, Pres dealt with the government housing at Oak Park and enlarged the building that served as the fire station, jail and city hall.

In 1939, Pres and Goodrich bought out Bob Swantner and renamed the company Heady Farm Machinery Co. They moved the business to a new building they'd built on US Highway 40 (East Pearce Boulevard). Early on, they realized the importance of offering a service department. By 1950, they had experienced rapid growth, and their sales had risen to six figures annually. They offered year-round employment to twelve to fifteen people. They also built a new building behind the Implement Company on Koenig.

Between 1944 and 1946, the brothers sold the eighty-acre farm west of town. They also sold Heady Hotel to Mary and Clem Obrecht and the Sinclair station on US 40. The Sinclair building today is a restaurant. When the brothers built the Implement Store, Pres and Alma also built a house next door on Talley. In 1945, they remodeled the home, adding a full basement and a living room.

Pres was elected president of the Wentzville Community Club in 1948, and in 1949, he served on the committee to try and establish a local police force. In 1950, Pres bought out Goodrich, who was starting to experience ill health. Goodrich died in 1957.

During these busy years, Preston loved to squirrel hunt.

Pres was nominated to run for mayor again in 1954 and lost to John Duello. In a three-way race, Pres came in dead last. Starting in 1956, Pres served on the board of the St. Charles County Fair. In 1958, he was elected president of the Wentzville Community Club for the second time. In earlier years, he was president for six years. During this time, the community club sold its property that was located on US 40 and bought the Musick property. Pres was frustrated by the lack of help from the community and wondered if the community club should disband. As of 2024, the Wentzville Community Club is still active.

In 1960, Pres sold the implement business to Jess Fletcher but retained ownership of the buildings. Also in 1960, he turned the building on Koenig into office and business space and the house on the corner of Koenig and Wall into rental property.

By 1964, Pres's health was not good. He had been in the hospital several times. But he bought the duplex on Carr from his sister-in-law Mollie Schierbaum's estate. Harvard Kessler had built the duplex after World

Preston Heady (*left*) squirrel hunting with Sam Anselm (*right*). *WCHS Collection.*

War II. The building is a concrete block building, and Harvard made each block by hand.

In September 1965, Alma died suddenly of heart failure. In December, Pres advertised for a live-in housekeeper. In January 1966, he announced his engagement to Rita Penman, a much younger woman who operated a beauty shop in Harvester. In May, Rita and Pres married. In 1966, he also sold the building that was home to the implement company, a shop building across the street on the south side of Pearce and his home. The sale allowed him to stay in the home on Talley until his death. Pres died on October 20, 1967. As you can see, he was instrumental in beginning many organizations and services we take for granted today.

Pres and Alma are buried in Linn Cemetery.

Gustavus "Gus" Temme

By Lois Kessler

Gustavus "Gus" Temme was born on January 27, 1899, and died on May 24, 1973. His parents were Heinrich Wilhelm Temme and Magdalena Neimeyer, who came to the United States from Germany. Gus's family moved to Wentzville when he was eighteen years old. In addition to Gus, the Temmes had five other children: Louis, William, Henry, Mamie and Lulu. Lulu died in 1912 after being ill for two days and was buried on the day she would have turned twenty-five. A special train went from Wentzville to Delmar Station and back for her funeral. Before moving to Wentzville, Gus's father was a gardener in the St. Louis area. His parents had a home and farm west of Wentzville. The home was torn down before 1975.

In August 1920, Gus started working with Gus Jungck at his harness shop. A couple of interesting notes about Jungck and his wife: in 1914, Gus Jungck ran for mayor but lost. In 1918, Mrs. Jungck and her friend Mrs. Sam McCoy walked from Wentzville to Washington, Missouri, a total of twenty-four miles. I'm not sure what time they left Wentzville, but they arrived in Washington, Missouri, at four o'clock in the afternoon.

In 1921, Gus bought the harness and shoe shop from Jungck. The year 1921 was a busy one, as Gus was also elected Wentzville city collector. He held this position until 1933.

On May 14, 1925, he married Alverda Emma Koenig in Greenburg, Kansas. Alverda's parents were Fred Koenig and Katherine Schermeier. Their first home was above the shoe shop, where they lived for four years.

From 1920 to '29, Gus Temme worked at his harness shop and shoe repair shop. *WCHS Collection.*

Gus and Alverda had two children: Roland Temme and Glenda Temme Gross. The Temme children and grandchildren were known for winning first prize in the annual WCC Homecoming Kiddie Parade.

Around 1929, Gus sold the harness shop to Fred Duello and moved his shoe repair shop to the short one-story building that is now part of the Smoke House restaurant. In 1933, a fire destroyed much of the shop's contents; the loss was estimated at between $800 and $1,000. The family moved to the Wullschleger house, which was located just east of the phone company building on East Main Street. The home was torn down before 1975. The family then moved to the John Koenig home, which was located on East Main on the eastern edge of the lot where the phone company building is on East Main Street.

In 1935, Gus bought the building that had been occupied by Dr. W.C. Caldwell and was owned by Ed S. Walker and Will Karrenbrock. The property had previously been owned by T.S. Thompson (who engaged in the tobacco industry). The building became known as the Gus Temme building and was located on West Main Street next to what is now known as Ellbee's General Store. The building was torn down in the mid-2000s. Gus had his shoe shop on the lower level, and the family lived upstairs. In 1945, there was a fire under the store of this building where Mr. Henke had a shoe shop. The damage was minimal, so Gus and Alverda continued to live upstairs until 1964.

In 1939, Gus was appointed justice of the peace of Cuivre Township, a position he held until 1941. As justice of the peace, he was the one who issued a murder warrant for Emma Hepperman in the death of Tony Hepperman. Gus resigned from the justice of the peace position in 1941, and A.L. Foltz was appointed to replace him. Gus resigned because he was appointed a state liquor inspector of the Missouri Department of Liquor, a position he held until his retirement on March 1, 1964. His first assignment, which lasted eighteen months, was Franklin, Gasconade, Crawford and Washington Counties. During this time, he and Alverda lived in Washington, Missouri, but Roland and Glenda stayed in Wentzville with relatives. After eighteen months, he was transferred to Lincoln, Pike, Warren, Montgomery and St. Charles Counties, so he and Alverda moved back to Wentzville.

In 1944, Gus's father, who was eighty-five years old, made the news because he claimed he was being poisoned. On his death, there was an autopsy and an inquest, and his internal organs were sent to the state highway patrol for testing. His claims were unfounded. But one must wonder if he had dementia and was recalling the poisoning case of Tony Hepperman.

Above: When Gus Temme was a young man, locomotives were a familiar sight in Wentzville, a railroad town. Here, Gus stands in front of a locomotive engine. *WCHS Collection.*

Left: Gus Temme was mayor of Wentzville in 1965 and 1966. *WCHS Collection.*

In February 1947, while on duty, Gus was in a drug store in St. Charles operated by Estella Wehmeier. While he was waiting for Wehmeier, another customer entered the store. When no one came to wait on Gus or the other customer, they went looking. They found Wehmeier in a storeroom, where she had been beaten to death with a blackjack. During the beating, the blackjack split open, and its contents were strewn across the floor. There was evidence of a struggle, and the cash register was empty.

On March 1, 1964, Gus retired from the state liquor inspection position, and in March 1964, he filed to run for mayor of Wentzville against Fred Payne. During his term as mayor, Fred had been involved in arguments and struggles with aldermen and city employees. Gus ran on a platform of getting along and cooperation. He won the election.

In 1965, the library board recommended that the Wentzville Library merge with the St. Charles County library system. Gus and the aldermen opposed this move because they thought the city would lose control of the library. While they were not wrong, the library board prevailed, and the Wentzville Library became part of the St. Charles County library system. The city also formed the first park board in 1965.

In 1964, Gus and Alverda built a new home on North Church Street. The home was located on the north side of Fireman's Park near center field. The property also had three or four trailers that the Temmes rented out. The house has since been torn down, and a subdivision is on the land.

Gus passed away on May 24, 1973. Alverda lived to ninety-five, passing away on January 26, 2003. Both are buried in South Linn Cemetery.

Bibliography

Books

Breslow, Lori. *Small Town.* John J. Buse Historical Museum, 1977.

Bryan, William S. *A History of the Pioneer Families of Missouri.* Bryan Brand and Company, 1876.

Corbett, Katharine T. *In Her Place: A Guide to St. Louis Women's History*. Missouri Historical Society Press, 1999.

Edom, Clifton, *Missouri Sketch Book.* Lucas Brothers, 1963.

1875 St. Charles County Illustrated Atlas Plat Book. W.R. Brink and Co. of Illinois, 1875.

Goodspeed, Weston Arthur. *The Province and the States: Robert Byron Dula*. Western Historical Association, 1904.

Guffey, Sheryl Kay. *Cottleville: Where History Never Grows Old—A Cottle Family Story*. 2nd ed. Trafford, 2017.

Long, W.B., and Barbara Long. *The Civil War Day by Day*. Doubleday, 1971.

Mallinckrodt, Anita M. *Why They Left: German Immigration from Prussia to Missouri.* Mallinckrodt Communications Research, 1992. Previously published in 1980.

The National Cyclopaedia of American Biography. Vol. 12. FB&c Ltd., Dalton House, 2018.

National Historical Company. *History of St. Charles, Montgomery and Warren Counties, Missouri.* National Historical Company, 1969. Previously published in 1885. Available at https://www.mdh.contentdm.oclc.org/digital/collection/mocohist/id/26291/ or https://archive.org/details/historyofstchar100nati/page/n9/mode/2up.

Niedner, Robert V., and William C. Goellner. *The Bridges at St. Charles, Missouri (The Saga of Man's Quest to Subjugate and Span the Missouri River, 1805–2003)*. Goellner Printing, 2003.

Rothwell, Dan A. *Along the Boone's Lick Road: Missouri's Contribution to Our First Transcontinental Route, U.S. Highway 40.* Young at Heart, 1999.

Trails West. National Geographic Society, 1983.

Waterworth, Edward. *The Makers of St. Louis: A Brief Sketch of the Growth of a Great City.* Legare Street Press, n.d.

Articles

Ancestry. "Find a Grave Index, 1600s–Current." https://www.ancestry.com.
Bales, Carol W. "Tobacco." *St. Charles County Business Record* (Wentzville, MO), March 27, 1958.
———. "Wentzville-One Time Tobacco Center." *Wentzville (MO) Union*, March 27, 1958.
The Bee (Danville, VA). "Caleb C. Dula Is Buried in New York City." December 27, 1930.
———. "Death Claims S.R. Dula at Hospital Here." July 10, 1930.
———. "Dula Left an Estate of $242,000." July 16, 1930.
———. "Mrs. J. C. Dula Fortune Left to Kinsmen." November 10, 1930.
Bonne Terre (MO) Register. "Sidney Dula-Guardian's Notice of Appointment." June 20, 1924.
Constam, Ike. "Wentzville: It's Growth and Progress." *St. Charles (MO) Weekly Cosmos-Monitor*, June 15, 1881.
Corpening, Albert N. "The Corpening Family (The Southern Branch)." Ancestry.com.
Daily Missouri Republican (St. Louis, MO). "Premium Sale of Missouri and Illinois Tobacco." June 16, 1866.
Denny, John. "A Short History of Wentzville, 1855–1955." *Official Program and Souvenir Wentzville Centennial and 21st Annual Homecoming*, September 3, 1955.
Detroit Free Press. "Pioneer Civil Engineer Erasmus L. Wentz Died at Bay City Yesterday." January 9, 1900.
E.L. Wentz and Company. "500 Men Wanted for Houston and Sabine Railroad." *St. Louis Globe-Democrat*, May 21, 1859.
Evening Mail (Stockton, CA). "C.C. Dulas Thoughts on Success." August 2, 1915.
Gates, Paul. "The Railroads of Missouri, 1850–1870." *Missouri Historical Review* 26, no. 2 (January 1932). https://digital.shsmo.org/digital/collection/mhr/id/12762/rec/3.
Inter Ocean (Chicago, IL). "The Drummond Tobacco Company." June 10, 1896.
Joplin (MO) News-Herald. "New Mining Companies." February 12, 1900.
Kansas City (MO) Times. "The Railroad News: Wentz Promotion." March 17, 1881.
Lenoir (NC) Topic. "Caldwell County's First Volunteers for the Confederate Service." May 13, 1896.
———. "Mr. and Mrs. L. W. English visiting." August 3, 1898.
Los Angeles Times. "L.W. English: His Condition Improved." May 21, 1906.
Malone, Ross. "Missouri's Earliest Forts and Fortresses." Unpublished presentation, St. Charles County Historical Society, 2024.
Matlock, Gerry. "A Look Back: Wentzville's First Store." *Messenger Tribune* (Wentzville, MO), January 4, 1964.
———. "From Whence Came Wentz." *St. Charles (MO) County Business Record*, July 21, 1976.
———. "History of West St. Charles County." *Messenger Tribune* (Wentzville, MO), October 19, 1977.
———. "Wentzville: The Railroad Town." *Past Times Saint Charles* 1, no. 2 (Summer 1984).
———. "William M. Allen: Founder of Wentzville." *Wentzville (MO) Union*, May 14, 1975.
Messenger and Intelligencer (Wadesboro, NC). "Death of Mr. George T. Dula Obituary." March 7, 1912.
Mexico Weekly Ledger (Mexico, MO). "Dula Success." August 5, 1915.
Missouriana. "Missouri Forts in the War of 1812." *Missouri Historical Review* 26, no. 3 (April 1932).
Mittlelbuscher, Barb, and Gerry Matlock. "The Great Tobacco Era of Western St. Charles County." *Past Times. St. Charles* 2, no. 2, 2nd Quarter (1985).
National Tribune (Washington, D.C.) "Battlefield Bibles." July 22, 1909.

New York Times. "Caleb C. Dula Dies; Tobacco Financier; Chairman of Board of Liggett & Myers Had Been President for Sixteen Years." December 26, 1930.

———. "R.B. Dula, Pioneer in Tobacco, Dead." April 28, 1926.

Olsen, Edna McElhiney. "Historical Series: Rudolph Goebel the Photographer." In *Historical Articles St. Charles, MO*, vol. 2. Richard G. Sperandio, 1990. Previously published in the *St. Charles Journal*, February 22, 1962.

Pearce, Benjamin, and S.W. Logan. "Sawing and Grinding Satisfactory Executed at the Wentzville Mill." *St. Charles (MO) Weekly Banner-News*, November 17, 1870.

Pearce, Benjamin C. "Notice Is Hereby Given, I Have Sold My Interest in the Firm of Evans, Pearce and Co." *Daily Missouri Republican* (St. Louis, MO), May 17, 1868.

Sandfort, Robert M. "Col. Arnold Krekel: Another Look at His Civil War Leadership." *Bulletin of the St. Charles County Historical Society* 33, no. 3 (July 2015).

Spirit of the Age (Raleigh, NC). "Sons of Temperance Brotherhood." September 21, 1853.

St. Charles (MO) County Business Record. "Woman Recovers Note Blown 70 Miles by Storm." July 23, 1915.

St. Charles (MO) Weekly Banner News. "L.W. English, Hawley-Murphy Trunk Co." August 7, 1902.

———. "Sheriff's Sale." March 2, 1871.

St. Charles (MO) Weekly Cosmos-Monitor. "C.E. Musick Funeral." July 24, 1929.

———. "Sidney Dula." August 15, 1900.

———. "The Wentzville Picnic." July 30, 1884.

St. Joseph (MO) Gazette, "Supervisor of Construction Wentz." March 17, 1881.

St. Louis (MO) Star and Times. "Head of $65,000,000 Corporation, Once a Tobacco Stripper, Tells Young Men How to Win Success." August 6, 1915.

St. Louis Globe-Democrat. "Adolphus Dula Obituary." April 21, 1912.

———. "L.W. English, Obituary." August 23, 1906.

———. "The Tornado Sufferers." May 26, 1883.

———. "Wedding at Wentzville." April 25, 1876.

St. Louis Post-Dispatch. "Name That Town." June 16, 1980.

———. "Society Belles of Wentzville." December 12, 1895.

———. "Trial of William F. Sharps." September 14, 1857.

———. "Well-Known St. Louisans." April 8, 1895.

The Sun (New York, NY). "Obituary: Erasmus L. Wentz." January 10, 1900.

Troy (MO) Herald. "Joseph Carter Goodrich." July 23, 1873.

Warrenton (MO) Banner. "Tobacco Kings." July 2, 1938.

Warrenton (MO) Herald. "Sidney Dula." September 26, 1899.

Wentzville (MO) Union. "William F. Karrenbrock Obituary." July 11, 1952.

Wisconsin Tobacco Reporter (Edgerton, WI). "Tobacco Antitrust Lawsuit." December 1, 1911.

Yonkers (NY) Statesman. "Dula Family Legal Notice." January 6, 1931.

Younkman, Tim. "Bay City Civil War Profile: E.L. Wentz." *Bay City (MI) Times*, April 9, 2011.

Government Sources

Bureau of Land Management. "U.S. General Land Office Records, 176-2015." Ancestry. https://www.ancestry.com.

Iowa Department of Public Health Bureau of Vital Records. "Iowa, U.S. Compiled Marriages, 1835–1850." Ancestry. https://www.ancestry.com.

Library of Congress. "U.S. City Directories, 1822–1995." Ancestry. https://www.ancestry.com.

Missouri Department of Vital Records. "Missouri, U.S. Marriage Records, 1805–2002." Ancestry. https://www.ancestry.com.

National Archives. *Bounty-Land Warrants for Military Service, 1775–1855.* July 2024. https://www.archives.gov/files/research/military/bounty-land-1775-1855.pdf.

National Park Service. "Civil War Info on Union Missouri Volunteers, 8th Regiment, Missouri Infantry." https://www.nps.gov/civilwar/search-battle-units-detail.htm?battleUnitCode=UMO0008RI.

National Register of Historic Places. "Wentzville Tobacco Company Factory." U.S. Department of the Interior, National Park Service, December 1990. https://mostateparks.com.

U.S. Army Civil War Provost Office. "English, Emma S—State: Virginia—Year: 1863." https://catalog.archives.gov/id/27739546?objectPages=5.

U.S. Census Bureau. "1840 United States Federal Census." Ancestry. https://www.ancestry.com.

———. "1850 United States Federal Census." Ancestry. https://www.ancestry.com.

———. "1860 United States Federal Census." Ancestry. https://www.ancestry.com.

———. "1860 United States Federal Census: Slave Schedules." Ancestry. https://www.ancestry.com.

———. "1870 United States Federal Census." Ancestry. https://www.ancestry.com.

———. "1880 United States Federal Census." Ancestry. https://www.ancestry.com.

———. "Missouri, U.S. Compiled Census and Census Substitutes Index, 1830–1860." Ancestry. https://www.ancestry.com.

Wentzville, Missouri. "History of Wentzville: The Beginnings." September 4, 2024. https://www.wentzvillemo.gov.

Websites and Blogs

Armentano, D.T. "Antitrust History: The American Tobacco Case of 1911." Foundation for Economic Education, March 1, 1971. https://fee.org/articles/antitrust-history-the-american-tobacco-case-of-1911.

Brail, Bob. "When Tobacco Was King in St. Charles County." *Just a Walk Down the Road: The History of Southern St. Charles County, Missouri* (blog), August 2017. http://justawalkdowntheroadblogspot.com.

Christensen, V.R. "The Dulas of Danville Tobacco." Old West End National Historic District, July 1, 2020. https://oldwestendva.com/blog/the-dulas-of-danville-tobacco.

Donovan, Mark. "Greystone: An Original 'Millionaires Row' Estate Is Home Still to the Mega Rich." July 27, 2021. https://markhistorydonovan.blogspot.com.

Great Rivers Greenway-Earth City Levee. March 2025. https://greatriversgreenway.org.

Historical Marker Database. "History of Wentzville, City of Wentzville Village Center, Inc. 1872." September 4, 2024. https://www.hmdb.org.

Koenig, R.R. "Sons of Johann Heinrich Koenig: Barkhausen to Wentzville." Ancestry.com, January 27, 2012.

North Missouri Railroad Company. March 2025. https://rootsweb.com.

Peckham Architecture, LLC. "Historic Downtown Wentzville Intensive Survey: April 7, 2022." September 4, 2024.

Wabash Railroad Historical Society. "About the Wabash Railroad (History)." July 2024. www.wabashrhs.org/p/wabash-railroad.html.

Index

C

D

E

F

G

H

I

J

N

O

P

Q

R

S

V

W

Z

About the Authors

Gerry Matlock received a BS in engineering from University of Missouri–Columbia. He was an engineer at McDonnell Douglas and Boeing in St. Louis, starting in 1968, for over thirty years. He was a founding member and president of the Wentzville Community Historical Society (WCHS) in 1974. While starting WCHS, he also wrote articles that were published in the *Wentzville Union* and the *Messenger Tribune*, which involved researching with families, community members and county and state offices.

Lois Kessler received a BA in general studies with minors in business, computer science and psychology. Her business career was in the insurance and trucking industries. She became president of WCHS in 2019 and in 2021 secured a space for the historical society museum and its archive, which she manages. She since has implemented the Annual Cemetery Tour and the Christmas Holiday Home Tour. She was selected as Wentzville Citizen of the Year in 2022. She serves on the Wentzville Downtown Committee and the boards of the Linn Cemetery Association and the Wentzville Community Club. She also manages the Wreaths Across America program for three cemeteries in Wentzville.

Kathy Weindel received a master's degree in social science and history from Tuman State University. She is a retired high school teacher from Francis Howell School District in St. Charles County. She taught American history and world history for thirty-one years. A resident of Wentzville, she volunteers at WCHS and does research for the society.